Copyright © 2023 Marie Anderson Publisher Ltd

All rights reserved. No part of this book may be reproduced or transmitted in any form or by any means, electronic or mechanical, including photocopying, recording, or by any information storage and retrieval system without permission in writing from the publisher. This book is designed to provide accurate and authoritative information in regard to the subject matter covered. It is sold with the understanding that the publisher and author are not engaged in rendering psychological, legal, or other professional services. If expert assistance is required, the services of a competent professional should be sought.

 Created with Vellum

WHISPERS OF CALM, A CHILD'S MEDITATION GUIDE

MEDITATION SERIES
BOOK 2

MANON DOUCET

EDITED BY **JENNIFER GERMANO**

EDITED BY **LAURIE DOUCET**

ILLUSTRATED BY **CLAIRE HOLBEIN**

ILLUSTRATED BY **MANON DOUCET**

ILLUSTRATED BY **FOSS PLUS**

ILLUSTRATED BY **GIANNA SALARIS**

"REVEAL THE QUIET MAGIC OF MINDFULNESS, GIFTING YOUR CHILD A SANCTUARY OF INNER PEACE."

A Guide for Parents and Caregivers
Discover the Marvels of Meditation as children, parents, and caregivers unlock the power to thrive in a busy world. Spark curiosity and uncover the tools needed for a balanced and fulfilling life.

By Manon Doucet

A voice for a new generation.

Manon Doucet delivers a breathtaking tour-de-force.

If you only read the books that everyone else is reading, you can only think what everyone else is thinking.

HARUKI MURAKAMI

Mindful Meditation is a must-read for parents and caregivers who want to support their children's mental and emotional well-being. With research-based insights, practical tips, and engaging stories and games, this book provides a roadmap for parents and caregivers to help their children develop essential life skills and thrive in today's world.

© 2023 Manon Doucet. All rights reserved.

Dedications.

*To the extraordinary souls who have shaped my journey,
This book stands as a testament to the unwavering support,
boundless love, and unyielding belief bestowed upon me by an
exceptional group of individuals. I extend my deepest appreciation
to Laurie and Jennifer, the dedicated editors whose expertise and
meticulous guidance have breathed life into these pages. Your
invaluable contributions have shaped the very essence of this work.*

I must also express my gratitude to Claire, Gianna, and myself, the brilliant illustrators who have adorned these words with captivating visuals. Through our artistic prowess, we have transformed the ideas and emotions within this book into vibrant, tangible images that enhance the reader's experience. Our creative collaboration has enriched the soul of this project.

To my father, daughter, and life partner, I owe immeasurable thanks. Your unwavering love and support have served as the cornerstone of my existence. Through the highs and lows, you have stood steadfastly by my side, providing encouragement and believing in me when doubt whispered in my ear. You are my guiding stars, forever illuminating my path.

A heartfelt acknowledgment also goes to my dear friends within the writing community. During moments of uncertainty and self-doubt, you have been pillars of support and voices of reason. Your unwavering faith in my abilities has emboldened me to persist and never succumb to the shadows of discouragement. Your presence in my life has been a constant reminder that I am never alone on this creative journey.

And to you, dear readers, who embark on this literary adventure alongside me, I dedicate this book with deep admiration. Within its pages lies the power to resonate deep within your soul, igniting your passions and empowering you to embrace the profound beauty of life's journey. May these words inspire you to reach beyond the limitations, conquer adversity, and wholeheartedly embrace the boundless possibilities life has to offer.
With immeasurable gratitude and boundless love,

Manon D.

FOREWORD

Hey there, and a big warm welcome to

"Meditation Adventures for Young Minds."

Meditation Made Easy for Children, nurturing well-being and thriving lives. I'm super excited to have you here, and I want to give a special shout-out to all the parents and caregivers who are all in when it comes to boosting their children's mental and emotional well-being.

In our world, which sometimes feels like it's moving at warp speed, helping our kids understand their emotions and thoughts can seem like climbing a steep mountain. But hey, don't sweat it! This book is your friend, your guide, here to help make meditation fun and approachable for your kids, laying down the stepping stones for a future filled with calmness, bounce-back-ability, and self-awareness.

Whether your kiddo is neurotypical, has ADHD, or is dealing with special needs, this book has got something for everyone. It offers down-to-earth techniques that can be tweaked to match their unique personalities and situations. As an author, I've spent heaps of time working hands-on with children from all walks of life, and I totally get the different needs and challenges they may encounter.

The great thing about meditation is that it's super simple, and kids can really get into it. In this book, my goal is to give you, the superheroes - parents and caregivers, the tools and know-how to nurture critical life skills in your kids. We're going to explore how to build focus and emotional control, develop empathy and self-confidence, and tap into the awesome transformative power of meditation.

Think of this book as your trusty sidekick on this journey. I'll walk you through step-by-step, share some wisdom nuggets, and provide practical exercises to help your kid build a strong well-being foundation. We're in this together, making sure that meditation becomes a fun and rewarding part of your lives.

Remember, you're not doing this alone. We're a community of parents and caregivers dedicated to shaping a future where our kids have the skills to handle life's curveballs with grace. Let's gear up our kids to thrive, grow, and discover their inner Zen in our ever-changing world.

So, take a moment, breathe in, open up, and let's get this journey started. Your child's well-being is worth every single step we take.

With warm wishes and gratitude,

Manon Doucet

CONTENTS

Prologue	1
Introduction to Mindful Meditation	5
Part 1: Understanding and Guiding Children's Emotions	7

1. UNDERSTANDING CHILDREN'S EMOTIONS — 9
An Essential Tool for Parents and Caregivers

Supporting Emotional Development in Children	9
The Importance of Emotional Development	10
Validating Children's Emotions	11
Teaching Emotional Literacy	12
Managing Difficult Emotions	13
Fostering Empathy and Perspective-Taking	14
The Magic of Play	14
Addressing Common Concerns	16
"Emo the Emotion Explorer"	19
"The Breathing Game"	29

2. CULTIVATING INNER PEACE IN CHILDREN. — 35
An Introduction to Mindfulness for Children

Why is Mindfulness Beneficial for Children?	37
How Can Children Practice Mindfulness?	40
Creating a Supportive Environment	42
Overcoming Potential Obstacles	43
"The Magical Forest"	47

3. TEACHING CHILDREN EFFECTIVE COMMUNICATION — 55
Empowering Children through Effective Communication

Teaching Emotional Awareness and Regulation	55
The Value of Emotional Awareness and Regulation	56
Fostering Emotional Awareness	57

Teaching Healthy Emotional Responses	59
Teaching Coping Skills	60
Building Resilience Through Play	63
Age-Specific Strategies	65
Infancy (0-1 year):	65
Toddlerhood (1-3 years):	66
Preschool (3-5 years):	66
School-age (6-12 years):	67
Creating a Compassionate Environment	68
Common Concerns	70
"The Emotion Express"	73

4. 4 CULTIVATING INNER PEACE TO RESOLVE OUTER CONFLICT — 81
Cultivating Inner Peace to Resolve Outer Conflict

Understanding Conflict's Root Causes	82
Managing Strong Emotions with Mindfulness	83
Communicating Needs with Mindful Clarity	84
Compassion, the Cornerstone of Conflict Resolution	86
Resolving Conflicts Collaboratively	87
Integrating Mindfulness Into Daily Life	88
"The Playground Problem Solvers"	91

5. CULTIVATING RESILIENCE AND SELF-REGULATION IN CHILDREN THROUGH MINDFULNESS — 97

Why Resilience Matters	97
Self-Regulation: A Cornerstone of Resilience	99
Infusing Mindfulness into Daily Life	99
Cultivating Resilience through Mindfulness	101
Composure promotes rational decision-making under pressure.	102
Self-Regulation Strategies	103
Brain Training for Resilience	105
Mindfulness Practices for Different Ages	106
Creating a Mindful Family Environment	109
Mindfulness Games for Building Resilience	110

Troubleshooting Common Obstacles	112
Conclusion	113
Part 2: Introducing Meditation to Children Through Stories	115

6. STORIES FOR CHILDREN TO HELP THEM UNDERSTAND MEDITATION TECHNIQUES — 117
Using Stories to Introduce Meditation to Children

The Power of Stories	117
Introducing Mindfulness Meditation	110
This story modeled:	120
Relaxation Through Storytelling	121
This story uses imagery to demonstrate:	122
Visualization for Inner Exploration	123
This story demonstrates how visualization can:	124
The Journey Ahead	125

7. INTRODUCING CHILDREN TO MEDITATION THROUGH ENCHANTING STORIES — 127

The stories we will highlight include:	127
"The Butterfly Garden: Where Magic Takes Flight"	131
"The Magic Forest: A Journey of Imagination"	139
"The Ocean Waves: A Relaxing Adventure"	145
A Special Note from Manon Doucet	153

8. MEDITATION THROUGH MORE ENCHANTING STORIES — 155
The stories we will highlight include:

"The Wise Tree"	159
"The Odyssey of the Mindful Voyager"	165
"The Magic Breath"	173
"The Rainbow of Emotions"	181
"The Gratitude Garden"	189
"The Ants"	195
"The Family Garden"	201
"The Mindful Explorer"	207
Part 3: Guiding Parents and Caregivers	213

9. STORIES FOR PARENTS AND CAREGIVERS TO HELP THEM WITH THEIR CHILDREN'S MEDITATION ... 215
Making Meditation Engaging and Relatable for Children
- Making It Playful ... 216
- Using Imagination ... 217
- Offering Diverse Techniques ... 218
- Options caregivers can provide include: ... 218
- Keeping it Short and Sweet ... 219
- Making it Social ... 220
- Celebrating the Journey ... 221
- The stories and exercises below provide a glimpse into making meditation child-friendly: ... 222
- Mindful Movement Meditation ... 223

10. GAMES FOR PARENTS AND CAREGIVERS TO HELP TEACH MEDITATION TECHNIQUES ... 225
    1. Mindful Scavenger Adventure: Explore with Your Senses! ... 226
    2. Breathing Buddies Adventure: Discover the Magic of Mindful Breathing! ... 227
    3. Musical Melodies: Journey into Mindful Listening! ... 229
    4. Joyful Journeys: Exploring Mindful Movement! ... 230
    5. Dreamy Adventures: Guided Visualization for Little Explorers! ... 232
    6. Magical Mindful Coloring: Where Art and Mindfulness Unite! ... 233
    7. Adventures in Earthing: Discovering the Magic Beneath Your Feet! ... 235
    - Here are more examples: ... 236

11. MINDFUL BREATHING AND OTHER EXERCISES ... 239
Journey into Mindfulness for Children
- Embarking on a Breathing Adventure: The 4-7-8 Breath Exercise ... 239
- Interactive Mindfulness Games and Activities ... 241

12. GUIDED MEDITATION EXERCISES *Rainbow Meditation: A Guided Meditation Exercise for Children*	243
Embarking on the Journey: Rainbow Meditation	243
Inhaling Colors: The Rainbow Journey	244
Conclusion of the Journey	246
Part 4: Practical Applications	247
13. CULTIVATING MINDFULNESS IN CHILDREN THROUGH DAILY PRACTICES	249
Why Daily Mindfulness Matters	250
Morning Mindfulness Practices	251
Bedtime Mindfulness Practices	253
Mealtime Mindfulness	254
Tailoring Mindfulness for Different Ages	257
Creating a Mindful Space	259
Troubleshooting Challenges	260
The Heart of the Matter: Loving-Kindness Practice	262
Conclusion	264
"The Colourful Journey: Mindful Colouring Adventures"	265
"The Whimsical Adventure of Muscle Relaxation"	271
"The Adventure of Sir Mindful: A Tale of Meditation and Mindfulness"	279
14. MAKING MINDFULNESS A JOYFUL FAMILY JOURNEY *Making Mindfulness a Joyful Family Journey*	285
Why Make It a Family Affair?	285
Tailoring Mindfulness: Ages and Stages	286
Setting the Stage for Success	287
Creative Mindfulness Activities for Families	288
Mindful Breathing Exercise	290
Journey into Mindfulness Through Poetry	290

15. GAMES FOR CHILDREN TO LEARN MEDITATION   295
Games and activities to teach children meditation techniques:
- Mindful Coloring   295
- Mindful Movement   296
- Mindful Breathing with Imagery   297
- Soothing Music and Mindful Listening   298
- Relaxing Body Scans   298
- Mindfulness through Nature   299
- Creative Arts and Crafts   300
- Practicing Kindness through Compassion Meditation   300
- Guided Relaxation and Visualization   301
- Relaxation through Squeezing Muscles   302
- Mindfulness Games and Exercises   302
- Mindfulness Meditation with Peers   303

- Meditation Magic: A Family's Path to Peace and Happiness   305
- Part 5: Establishing Mindfulness as a Lifestyle   313

16. OVERCOMING HURDLES IN TEACHING MEDITATION TO CHILDREN   315
- The Resistance Battle   315
- Confronting Discomfort   316
- Understanding the Abstract   317
- Overcoming Obstacles in Teaching Meditation to Children   318
- Conquering Resistance   318
- Addressing Discomfort   319
- Simplifying Complexity   319
- Unlocking the Power of Meditation for Children   320
- The Path of Engagement   321
- The Journey of Progression   321
- The Power of Community   322
- Unleashing the Power of Meditation for Children   323
- Embracing Emotional Well-being   323
- Boosting Cognitive Development   323
- Fostering Social Skills   324

The Journey Continues	324
Nurturing Harmony in Teaching Meditation to Children	325
Cultivating Collaboration	325
Modeling Positive Practices	325
Creating a Safe Space	326
Resistance to Meditation: Addressing Power Imbalances	327
The Collaborative Path	327
Coercion and Manipulation: Fostering Resistance	329
Lack of Agency: Nurturing a Sense of Empowerment	331
Collaborative Approach: Honoring Choices and Preferences	334
Modeling Positive Behavior: Leading by Example	334
Creating a Safe Space: Trust and Open Communication	336
Flexibility and Adaptability: Tailoring Meditation to Individual Needs	339
Conclusion	341
Nurturing Empowerment and Growth in Teaching Meditation to Children	341

17. TEACHING MEDITATION TO CHILDREN FROM DIVERSE CULTURES — 345
    Q&A
    Part 6: Addressing Questions and Challenges — 357

18. CONCLUSION AND NEXT STEPS: EMBRACING MINDFULNESS IN EVERYDAY LIFE — 359
    Conclusion: Continuing Our Mindfulness Journey
    Looking Ahead With Mindful Intention — 362
    Conclusion: A Mindfulness Seed Planted With Love — 362

Afterword	365
Also by Manon Doucet	369
References	371
A Special Note from Manon Doucet	383
About the Author	385

PROLOGUE
UNLEASHING THE POWER OF MINDFUL MEDITATION FOR CHILDREN

YOU KNOW how it is these days - our kids are up against a whole lot more than we ever were. Homework, soccer practice, piano lessons, and don't even get me started on social media. It's no wonder they're feeling stressed out and disconnected. It's a tough world for our young ones, and it's not always easy for us as parents and caregivers, either.

Here's the thing; we want our kids to grow up happy, healthy, and able to roll with life's punches. But the truth is, they're dealing with a bunch of challenges we never had to face when we were their age. And the digital age? It's a double-edged sword. Sure, they've got the world at their fingertips, but they're also bombarded with distractions, struggling to focus, and feeling all kinds of pressure that we can only imagine. We know stress takes a toll on us as adults, and it's no different for our kids.

. . .

But don't worry - there's a secret weapon we can give them. It's called mindful meditation, and it can be a real game-changer. Mindful meditation is all about getting our kids to slow down, take a breath, and really soak in the here and now, minus the judgment. It's a way to help them cool their jets, handle their feelings, and find that quiet place inside where everything's just... peaceful.

Think about it: what if we could give our kids the gift of mindfulness from an early age? Imagine them growing up with the ability to understand their own emotions, to deal with life's curveballs with clarity and compassion, and not get swept away by every storm. That's what mindful meditation can do.

You know the science backs this up, right? Mindful meditation can help reduce stress and anxiety, improve focus and self-control, and boost things like empathy and self-esteem. It even strengthens those brain connections linked to emotional health and resilience. And let's be honest - in a world where kids' mental health issues are on the rise, we need all the help we can get.

So, here's where this book comes in. I've written this to be a comprehensive, easy-to-follow guide to introduce mindful meditation to kids from as young as newborns right up to 22. But don't worry - everyone else can benefit too. I've poured the best research, real-life examples, and my own experience into practical tips and clear instructions that I hope will make introducing meditation to your kids a breeze.

. . .

Let's explore how we can teach our kids important skills like emotional regulation, effective communication, and even conflict resolution. And the best part? It won't be boring. You'll find engaging stories and games that will make meditation feel more like fun than a chore, and your kids will learn how to use meditation as a tool to handle their emotions, boost their focus, and just feel good about themselves.

Consider this book your go-to resource. By embracing mindful meditation and practicing it regularly, you can help your kids navigate today's tough world with inner strength and resilience.

So, let's get started on this journey together. Ready to discover the power of mindful meditation for kids? I hope so. Let's go!

INTRODUCTION TO MINDFUL MEDITATION
THE BIG IDEA BEHIND THIS BOOK: MAKING MEDITATION FUN FOR KIDS AND PARENTS!

The purpose of this book is to provide a valuable resource that introduces meditation to children and parents in an engaging and interactive way. We understand that teaching mindfulness to children can sometimes be challenging, which is why we have crafted this book to make the process enjoyable and accessible for both children and their parents.

Within the pages of this book, you will find a collection of stories, games, and activities designed to introduce meditation to children in a fun and relatable manner. These stories and games serve as stepping stones, guiding children on a journey of self-discovery and inner peace.

Through the power of storytelling, children will embark on imaginative adventures, exploring themes of mindfulness, kindness, gratitude, and compassion. The stories will not only captivate their attention but also provide them with valuable life lessons and practical tools they can apply in their daily lives.

Accompanying the stories are interactive games and activities that encourage active participation from both children and parents. These games are designed to make the learning process enjoyable and interactive, fostering a sense of connection and shared experience between parents and their children.

We believe that introducing meditation to children should be a collaborative effort between parents and their little ones. That's why this book includes guidance and tips for parents, offering support and insight into how to facilitate their child's meditation practice best.

By engaging with the stories, games, and activities in this book, parents and children can embark on a journey together, discovering the benefits of mindfulness and meditation in a way that is meaningful and enjoyable for the whole family.

Our aim is to empower children with valuable life skills while fostering a deeper connection and understanding between parents and their children. We hope that this book becomes a treasured resource in your family, helping you create moments of calm, joy, and growth through the practice of meditation.

PART 1: UNDERSTANDING AND GUIDING CHILDREN'S EMOTIONS

Understanding Children's Emotions
    "Emo the Emotion Explorer"
    "The Breathing Game"
    Cultivating Inner Peace in Children
    "The Magical Forest"
    Teaching Children Effective Communication
    "The Emotion Express"
    Cultivating Inner Peace to Resolve Outer Conflict
    "The Playground Problem Solvers"
    Cultivating Resilience and Self-Regulation in Children through Mindfulness

CHAPTER 1
UNDERSTANDING CHILDREN'S EMOTIONS
AN ESSENTIAL TOOL FOR PARENTS AND CAREGIVERS

SUPPORTING EMOTIONAL DEVELOPMENT IN CHILDREN

AS CHILDREN GROW and interact with the world around them, they experience a diverse range of emotions - joy, sadness, fear, anger, and everything in between. Learning to understand and manage this emotional landscape is a key developmental task of childhood. When equipped with strong emotional regulation skills, children gain the ability to handle life's ups and downs, resilience, and navigate social complexities.

In this chapter, we explore practical strategies for nurturing emotional intelligence in children. We provide guidance on how to create an environment that validates children's feelings, teaches emotional literacy through modeling and activities, and leverages the power of play to foster socio-emotional growth. Our aim is to provide parents and caregivers with actionable tools to help children cultivate self-awareness, express themselves constructively, and form meaningful connections with others.

THE IMPORTANCE OF EMOTIONAL DEVELOPMENT

> "Emotional development refers to the ability to understand, express, and manage feelings at different stages of life and to cope with the challenges along the way" (Hayman & Coleman, 2016)

Emerging research has demonstrated just how critical emotional aptitude is for children's overall well-being and success.

On a neuroscientific level, emotional regulation relies on connections between the amygdala, the brain's emotional center, and the prefrontal cortex, which governs executive functions.

> "Studies show that skills like problem-solving, focus, and impulse control depend heavily on the strength of connections between these two areas," notes a neuropsychologist (Clauss-Ehlers et al., 2020).

Activities that reinforce these neural links support cognitive, social, and behavioural development.

Additionally, researchers have found that emotional intelligence - the ability to understand and express feelings effectively - is pivotal for forming and sustaining social relationships.

A meta-analysis by researcher Dr. Marc Brackett (2019) concluded that children with higher emotional aptitude exhibit greater empathy, friendship skills, confidence, and morality compared to peers with lower aptitude.

Given the array of benefits, nurturing emotional skills during childhood is just as essential as fostering intellectual abilities. Fortunately, there are many engaging and enjoyable ways parents and caregivers can help children develop emotional intelligence.

VALIDATING CHILDREN'S EMOTIONS

The first step is creating an environment where children feel safe expressing their full range of emotions. Children often absorb subtle cues from adults about which feelings are acceptable or unacceptable to show. For example, responding with dismissal or punishment when a child expresses anger teaches them to suppress this emotion.

> "Validating children's emotions, without judgment, makes them feel understood and builds trust" (Review et al., 2018).

He suggests using empathetic listening strategies:
• Offer your full attention when a child shares difficult feelings such as fear or frustration. Avoid interrupting or downplaying their experience.
• Paraphrase what they share to show you understand.

> "It sounds like you feel very let down that your friend didn't come to your birthday party. That must be really disappointing."

- Resist the urge to immediately **"fix"** the situation. Allow them space to express themselves fully without jumping into problem-solving mode.
- Avoid criticizing the emotion. Rather than saying,

> "Stop being so angry about your lost toy,"

you could say,

> "I see you are really angry. I understand why you feel that way. Let's talk about what we can do to find your toy."

Through consistent emotional validation, children learn to become attentive to their feelings, understand the different emotions they experience, and express themselves constructively without fear of judgment.

TEACHING EMOTIONAL LITERACY

Emotional literacy is the ability to identify and name different feelings. Parents can foster this skill through modeling:

- Verbalize your own feelings:

> "I'm feeling a bit worried about Grandma being sick."

- Attach feeling words to their experiences:

> "You seem really excited about your friend's party!"

- Ask open questions:

  > "How did you feel when you got that special art award?"

- Discuss characters' emotions in books and shows:

  > "Look at his face - he seems really surprised about the talking dog!"

Expand your child's emotional vocabulary by providing diverse feeling words like amused, proud, grateful, relieved, embarrassed, and cranky. Also, use face charts or emoji cue cards to practice matching facial expressions with feeling words. Not only does this build self-awareness, but it equips children to recognize others' unspoken emotions through body language and facial cues.

MANAGING DIFFICULT EMOTIONS

When children grapple with challenging emotions like anger, sadness, or fear, teach them healthy coping strategies:
- Breathe deeply
- Take a break from the situation
- Talk it through or write feelings down
- Release emotions through safe physical outlets like pillow punching or exercise
- Use calming techniques like stretching, listening to music, coloring

Avoid reacting punitively to outbursts since this causes children to suppress, rather than process, difficult feelings. Staying patient and guiding them to work through emotions adaptively strengthens their self-regulation skills. Affirm their efforts by saying,

> "I'm proud of you for finding a calm way to manage your frustration."

FOSTERING EMPATHY AND PERSPECTIVE-TAKING

A key aspect of emotional intelligence is appreciating other perspectives. We can nurture this by discussing how characters in books feel, prompting children to consider others' needs during playtime, or having them reflect on how their actions impact the people around them. Asking open-ended questions like

> "How do you think she felt when you took her toy?"

Encourages children to see beyond their own viewpoint.

By walking children through understanding others' feelings and being kind, caring, and respectful, we impart compassion and empathy - feelings that will come to define their moral character.

THE MAGIC OF PLAY

Play serves as a wonderful avenue for children to explore their expanding emotional landscape.

> "Play allows kids to express feelings, experiment with different emotional responses, and gradually master their emotions." (Sanders & Morawska, 2018)

Child development expert agrees: "Play is really the work of childhood. It's very purposeful. It helps children learn to regulate their feelings and behavior. Through play, kids learn to handle anxiety, move through conflicts, and build self-confidence." (*The Advocate,* 2001)

Here are some examples of play activities that support emotional development:
- Dress-up characters and act out emotional scenarios
- Create imaginary worlds where stuffed toys experience different feelings
- Draw pictures or build scenes from clay to represent an emotion
- Make up skits or songs with family members about feelings
- Mold play dough faces into different emotional expressions
- Invent new feelings with made-up names like **"the wiggles"** or **"the grumbles."**

Remember, play should be child-led rather than adult-directed. Allow children to take the reins in inventing emotional narratives instead of scripting stories for them. Spontaneous play enables authentic self-expression and emotional exploration.

By incorporating play regularly in your child's routine, you provide an outlet for learning critical skills like communicating needs, managing impulses, cooperating with others, and tolerating frustration. Play is the training ground where emotional intelligence takes root.

ADDRESSING COMMON CONCERNS

As you strive to nurture your child's emotional skills, some common concerns may arise:

- **"My child has big feelings and frequent emotional outbursts."** Remember, this is developmentally normal. Focus on teaching them constructive ways to cope when upset. Stay calm and provide love through their ups and downs.
- **"When I validate my child's feelings, it seems to reinforce their tantrums."** Offer empathy while still maintaining reasonable boundaries. You might say,

> "I understand you want that toy. It's hard when you can't have something you want. We can look for another toy that's similar."

- **"My child is struggling socially and seems unable to understand peers' feelings."** Role-play various social scenarios to practice perspective-taking. Also, arrange play dates with slightly older children who can model emotional skills.
- **"I'm overwhelmed by my own feelings. How can I teach emotional skills?"** Remember, parenting is a learning journey, and we all have areas for growth when it comes to emotions. Don't hesitate to seek support from counselors or parenting groups. Addressing our own emotional needs makes us better equipped to guide our children.

With sensitivity, patience, and consistency using the strategies above, your child will flourish emotionally. Keep in mind skills like self-regulation take years to fully develop - our role is to gradually build their capabilities over time. If you have any concerns about your child's emotional health, don't hesitate to consult a child psychologist.

Conclusion

In summary, validating children's emotions, expanding their emotional vocabulary, teaching coping strategies for difficult feelings, fostering perspective-taking, and incorporating play provide the building blocks for strong emotional aptitude. These abilities allow children to understand themselves deeply, relate to others meaningfully, and lead more fulfilling lives. By making emotional intelligence a central goal from a young age, we can raise children who are self-aware, resilient, socially adept, and ethically grounded. Our children's emotional well-being and success rest on the foundations we help them build and the emotional connection we share with them.

"EMO THE EMOTION EXPLORER"
STORYTIME:

© 2023 Foss Plus. All rights reserved.

"Emo the Emotion Explorer"

One bright morning, Emo the emoji hopped out of bed, bubbling with excitement.

> "Today's the day!"

He shouted. Today, Emo was embarking on an adventure to

explore Emotopia, the magical realm of emotions. He loaded his yellow backpack with snacks and necessities and started his journey.

After bidding goodbye to his family, Emo set off on his journey. His first stop was the Silly Forest, an enchanting place filled with towering, chuckling trees. As Emo walked through the forest, he heard a chorus of laughter echoing from above. Looking up, he saw a group of monkeys frolicking on the branches, pulling goofy faces, and hanging upside down by their tails.

> "Wow! You monkeys sure know how to have a good time!"

Exclaimed Emo, looking up at their shenanigans.

One monkey, wearing a banana peel as a hat, swung down from a branch and landed with a soft thud beside Emo.

> "Well, life is more fun when you're laughing! Care to join us, Emo?"

The monkey said, holding out a banana peel hat to him.

Emo laughed, put on the banana peel hat, and said,

> "Why not? Let's make today super silly!"

Emo and the monkeys spent the whole morning pulling faces, trying to outdo each other with the funniest expressions they could muster. They laughed, chased each other, and played hide and seek. Amidst the fun, the banana-hat monkey called everyone for a break.

> "Let's play another game now, Emo. It's called; The Breathing Balloon."

The monkey explained.

Everyone gathered in a circle, with Emo in the middle. The monkey continued,

> "Close your eyes and imagine a balloon in your belly. Now, when you breathe in, picture the balloon inflating, getting bigger and bigger. Then, as you breathe out, the balloon slowly deflates. Ready to give it a try?"

Emo and the monkeys spent the next few moments quietly, inhaling and exhaling, picturing their breathing balloons. Emo found it to be a relaxing break from all the silliness. Even in the midst of their laughter and games, the monkeys had found a way to be calm and mindful.

Once they finished their **'Breathing Balloon'** game, Emo thanked the monkeys for the fun morning and the relaxation exercise.

> "Thanks, friends! I'll definitely take this funny silliness and peaceful meditation with me on my journey."

With a heart full of joy and a mind calm from the meditation, Emo continued his adventure, leaving the sounds of giggles and rustling leaves behind.

After leaving the laughter-filled Silly Forest, Emo's path led him to the entrance of a gloomy place known as the Sad Cave. As he ventured deeper into the cave, he heard soft sniffling sounds echoing off the stone walls. Turning a corner, he found a tiny lion cub curled up, his small body shaking with sobs.

> "What's wrong, little lion?"

Emo asked, his voice filled with concern.

> "I lost my family."

The cub whimpered, his eyes brimming with tears.

> "We were playing hide and seek, and now I can't find them anywhere."

> "Don't worry, we'll find them."

Emo reassured the cub. He held the little lion's paw and added, "But first, let's try something to help you feel a little better. It's a type of meditation called **'The Loving-Kindness Wish.'"**

Intrigued, the lion cub wiped his tears and looked at Emo.

> "How do we do that?"

Emo explained,

> "First, close your eyes. Picture yourself in your mind and say. May I be safe, may I be happy, may I be healthy, may I live with ease.' Now, think of your parents. Picture them in your mind and send them the same wishes."

The lion cub followed Emo's guidance. As he repeated the wishes, his sobs slowly subsided, replaced by calm, steady breaths. They continued the Loving-Kindness meditation for a few more minutes, sending good wishes to each other, their friends, and even those who weren't present.

> "Now, let's find your family."

Emo said, rising to his feet. He kept a gentle hold of the lion cub's paw, and together, they called out for the cub's parents.

Eventually, they heard a distant

> "Roar!"

And followed it until they found the lost lion cub's parents. The reunion was touching, filled with relieved roars, warm nuzzles, and a group hug. The lions thanked Emo and even invited him to join their game of hide-and-seek.

As Emo bid farewell to his lion friends, he felt content, knowing he had not only helped reunite a family but also taught a young lion how to find calm and send out positive wishes in moments of distress. With the experience etched in his heart, he was ready to continue his adventure in Emotopia. Before leaving the cave, he drew a cheerful face on the wall, hoping to uplift the next visitor.

Back on the trail, Emo skipped until he arrived at Play Park. There, he saw animals playing and expressing all kinds of emotions.

A frustrated fox sat under a tree, struggling with his shoelaces. His paws fumbled, tangling the laces into knots.

> "Don't get upset."

Emo advised.

> "I can assist you."

Patiently, he demonstrated how to loop the laces. Soon, the fox's shoes were neatly tied.

> "Thanks, Emo!"

Fox exclaimed, visibly happier.

Nearby, a delighted hippo was laughing while sliding down the twisting slide.

> "Wheee!"

He hollered as he splashed into the pool.

Emo giggled and climbed up to take a turn.

> "Here I go!"

He shouted as he slid down.

Just as Emo was about to leave Play Park, he heard a loud commotion. Turning around, he saw an angry alligator causing quite a scene at the dessert stand.

> "All the ice cream's gone."

The vendor explained patiently,

> "I'm sorry, Mr. Alligator, but there's none left."

But the alligator wasn't having it. He stomped his foot and roared,

> "I want more ice cream!"

Emo stepped up, his face calm, and gently placed a hand on the alligator's shoulder.

> "Hey, Mr. Alligator,"

Emo began,

> "I see you're really upset. It's okay to feel angry, but let's try to handle it in a better way."

The alligator snorted, crossing his arms over his chest.

> "And how do I do that?"

> "By practicing mindfulness,"

Emo explained.

> "It's about paying attention to what's happening right now without judgment. Let's try a technique called 'Take Five.' It's easy and can help you feel better."

The alligator looked at him curiously, so Emo continued,

> "Put your hand up like a star. Now, with your other hand's index finger, start tracing the outline of your star hand. As you go up each finger, take a deep breath in. As you go down each finger, breathe out. Do this for your whole hand."

As the alligator followed Emo's guidance, he felt his anger start to cool. He focused on his breaths and the sensation of his finger tracing his hand. His clenched jaw relaxed, and his rigid posture loosened.

Once they finished, Emo pulled out a spare ice cream cone from his backpack.

> "Now, how about we share this ice cream? It's not much, but it's something."

The alligator gave him a grateful smile, accepting the ice cream.

> "Thanks, Emo, and thanks for the 'Take Five' thing. It actually helped."

He said, his voice much calmer.

Pleased to have introduced mindfulness and eased a tough situation, Emo continued his journey through the magical land of Emotopia, ready for more adventures.

Emo spent the day playing with his new friends. He slid down slides, swung on swings, and learned that listening and sharing could help manage difficult emotions.

After a long day of adventuring, Emo was feeling quite tired. His legs ached from hopping through Silly Forest, and his voice was raspy from yelling in Sad Cave.

As the sun began to set over Emotopia, Emo knew it was time to return home. He followed the path out of Play Park and back through the colorful woods.

Up ahead, Emo saw his small cottage exactly as he had left it. He went inside, changed into his comfiest pajamas, and climbed into his cozy bed.

The blankets felt so soft and warm around him. He nestled his head into his pillow and let out a big yawn. Emo pondered the emotions he had experienced that day - silliness, sadness, frustration, joy. He was excited about the new feelings that awaited him in tomorrow's adventure.

With thoughts of laughing monkeys, rescued lions, and new friends dancing in his mind, Emo's eyes fluttered shut. He snuggled deeper into the covers and quickly drifted off to sleep, recharging for another thrilling day in the magical world of Emotopia.

The END

"THE BREATHING GAME"
STORYTIME:

© 2023 Foss Plus. All rights reserved.

"The Breathing Game"

Once upon a time, in a cozy little house filled with laughter, there lived a vibrant young girl named Emily. Emily adored games of all kinds - board games, jumping rope, freeze tag, you name it! But her absolute favorite was when her mom would make up a new game just for the two of them to play.

One sunny Saturday morning, Emily bounded down the stairs

to find her mom waiting in the living room with a playful twinkle in her eye.

> "Good morning, sunshine! I have a super fun new game for us to try today."

She said, patting the spot on the floor next to her.

Emily's face lit up. She loved their special mom-and-me games more than anything.

> "A new game? Awesome!"

Emily cheered, plopping down cross-legged.

> "What's this one called?"

> "It's called...the Breathing Game!"

Her mom declared. Then she took an exaggerated deep breath in through her nose, expanding her chest, before slowly breathing out through pursed lips.

Emily tilted her head curiously.

> "We're going to breathe?"

She asked. That didn't sound as exciting as their games of Hopscotch Town or Lava Monster.

Her mom nodded enthusiastically.

> "That's right! But not just regular breathing. We're going to take really deep, slow breaths together and see how it makes us feel. Here, just watch me first."

She proceeded to demonstrate another cycle of breathing -

inhaling smoothly and deeply through her nose, shoulders rising, then steadily exhaling out her mouth while deflating her chest.

> "Your turn now."

> "Big breath in..."

She encouraged Emily. Emily mimicked her mom, inhaling deeply and feeling her lungs fill up.

> "And out..."

She pursed her lips, exhaling slowly like she was blowing out birthday candles. Hmm, this did feel strangely calming.

> "How was that, Mom?"

Emily asked.

> "You're a natural breathing pro!"

Her mom cheered.

> "Now, let's keep going. I bet we can get to 100 breaths!"

Emily loved a challenge.

> "You're on!"

She cried, and so the Breathing Game commenced, Emily and her mom sitting cross-legged, eyes closed, syncing their rhythmic inhale and exhales. Emily felt her shoulders relax as oxygen circulated through her body.

In...2...3...out...2...3...in...2...3...out...2...3.

Their breaths fell into a steady cadence, like the soothing sound of ocean waves. Emily's mind began to clear, losing track of any worrisome thoughts.

By breath 25, Emily noticed the sunlight's warmth on her face as it streamed through the window. By breath 50, she heard neighborhood birds chorusing outside. And by breath 75, an inner sense of calm washed over her as if she were floating on a fluffy cloud.

Finally, they completed their 100th belly breath. Emily's eyes fluttered open, her whole body buzzing with energy yet feeling tranquil at the same time.

"Whoa...I feel amazing!"

She remarked.

"It's like I just took a super chill nap or something."

Her mom laughed.

"Right? Deep breathing is so calming for both the body and mind. It's one of my favorite daily wellness tools."

"Can we play again tomorrow?"

Emily asked hopefully. This Breathing Game was her new favorite, even more fun than freeze tag.

"Absolutely!"

Her mom replied, giving her a hug.

> "We can play this anytime you want. Deep breaths are always there when you need to find your center."

From then on, Emily practiced her breathing game often, whether sitting at her desk at school, waiting in line, or lying in bed before sleep. A few deep breaths could smooth out a stressful moment like magic.

One night, Emily woke from a nightmare, heart pounding. But a few minutes of breathing in and out helped lull her back to sleep.

Another day, she fell and scraped her knee at the playground. The breathing game soothed her tears.

At her piano recital, when nerves threatened to sabotage her performance, a few centering breaths reminded her that she had prepared, helping her master the piece.

Soon, Emily decided to share her special calming game with her best friend, Lucy, who often got nervous about tests at school.

> "It's easy! Just breathe in really slowly through your nose, like you're smelling your favorite flower. Then breathe out gently through your mouth. We'll do it together."

As they sat side by side, breathing in unison, Lucy's shoulders untensed.

> "Wow, I can feel my stress melting away!"

She said in amazement.

From then on, Emily and Lucy practiced their breathing game together before exams or presentations, filling their lungs with confidence and clarity.

One afternoon, Emily's mom walked by her room to see both

girls sitting serenely, eyes closed, chests rising and falling with graceful breaths. Emily peeked one eye open.

> "We're playing the Breathing Game, Mom! I taught Lucy, and now it's helping her not feel so nervous about stuff. Breathing is like magic!"

She exclaimed.

Her mom smiled proudly. At 10 years old, Emily discovered a skill it took some people decades to unlock.

> "You're so right, my dear. You've found one of life's greatest secrets - the power lies within your own breath."

She said with a wink.

Emily beamed back. She couldn't wait to share her magical breathing game with even more people, helping them tap into the superpower that had been inside them all along.

The End.

CHAPTER 2
CULTIVATING INNER PEACE IN CHILDREN.
AN INTRODUCTION TO MINDFULNESS FOR CHILDREN

IN TODAY'S FAST-PACED WORLD, children face numerous pressures that can lead to stress, anxiety, and emotional turmoil. As parents and caregivers, it is our responsibility to equip children with effective tools to navigate challenges, manage emotions, and cultivate inner peace. This is where mindfulness comes in.

> Mindfulness is the practice of focusing one's awareness on the present moment with openness, curiosity, and acceptance (Eddy & Moradian, 2018)

When applied skillfully, it can profoundly benefit children's overall well-being and development. In this introductory chapter, we will explore the fundamentals of mindfulness, its significance for children, and the scientifically-proven benefits it offers. By gaining a deeper understanding of mindfulness, you will be equipped with the knowledge to guide children in cultivating tranquility and emotional balance.

What is Mindfulness?

Mindfulness teaches children to direct their attention to the present moment rather than dwelling on the past or worrying about the future.

> According to psychologists, mindfulness is "paying attention to the present moment with care, curiosity, and kindness" (Bethune, 2023).

This involves tuning into one's thoughts, feelings, and bodily sensations without judgment.

Mindfulness differs from meditation in that it can be applied broadly in everyday life, not just during formal practice.

> As a world-renowned mindfulness expert explains, "Mindfulness is awareness, cultivated by paying attention in a sustained and particular way: on purpose, in the present moment, and non-judgmentally" (Welch, 2020).

Whether children are playing, learning, conversing, or even eating, they can practice paying close attention with an attitude of openness.

. . .

The aim of mindfulness is not to empty the mind or avoid one's thoughts and emotions. Instead, it teaches children to observe their inner experiences with curiosity and accept them without criticism. This builds emotional awareness and equips them to respond wisely rather than react impulsively.

> Adopting a mindful approach empowers children to consciously choose their actions and behaviors (Kenrick, 2018)

WHY IS MINDFULNESS BENEFICIAL FOR CHILDREN?

Incorporating mindfulness into children's daily routines offers myriad benefits that extend across their physical, mental, social, and emotional realms. Extensive research over the past few decades highlights the positive impact of mindfulness on children's development and well-being.

> On a neuroscientific level, mindfulness strengthens children's executive functioning, which includes skills like planning, focus, organization, and impulse control. Studies show that mindfulness practices activate the prefrontal cortex, the area of the brain responsible for executive function (*Issues in Clinical Psychology, Psychiatry, and Counseling: 2011 Edition*, 2012).

Enhanced executive skills lead to improved concentration, learning, and goal-directed behaviors.

. . .

Mindfulness has also been shown to reduce anxiety and depression symptoms in children by modifying their emotional regulation.

> A meta-analysis of 24 studies with over 2000 child participants found that mindfulness-based interventions significantly decreased anxiety, depression, stress, and negative emotions (*Issues in Pediatric and Adolescent Medicine Research and Practice: 2011 Edition*, 2012b)

Children become more adept at managing difficult feelings constructively rather than being overwhelmed by them.

Furthermore, mindfulness cultivates self-awareness as children learn to tune into their inner experiences.

> This builds their capacity for reflection and discernment when responding to external situations (Stanley et al., 2018b)

Rather than reacting impulsively, children can pause, tune inward, and make conscious choices aligned with their needs and values.

The benefits of mindfulness extend beyond children's inner emotional landscapes to their social skills and relationships.

Studies demonstrate that mindful children have greater empathy, altruism, tolerance, and patience toward others compared to their non-mindful counterparts (Congress, 1974).

By stabilizing their own emotions, mindful children become more capable of recognizing others' feelings and needs more accurately.

Mindfulness also enhances children's self-esteem and body image through self-acceptance and letting go of self-criticism (Hay, 2016).

Children learn to appreciate themselves just as they are, with all their quirks and imperfections. This promotes overall well-being and resilience even in the face of setbacks or challenges.

In summary, mindfulness empowers children with critical life skills that enable them to:

- Regulate emotions and manage stress constructively
    - Strengthen concentration, learning, and executive function
    - Build self-awareness and reflection
    - Develop social skills like empathy and compassion
    - Foster positive self-esteem and body image
    - Cultivate resilience in the face of life's challenges

. . .

The earlier children are exposed to mindfulness, the greater the benefits.

Neuroplasticity is highest in childhood as the brain rapidly develops neural connections (Chen et al., 2014).

Mindfulness helps guide the brain's growth in positive directions that will support self-regulation and healthy development across their lifespan.

HOW CAN CHILDREN PRACTICE MINDFULNESS?

Mindfulness techniques can be adapted appropriately for children depending on their age and abilities. Some examples of child-friendly mindfulness practices include:

Mindful breathing - Have children focus on the sensations of breathing. Watch the breath as it enters and leaves the nose. Place a hand on the belly and feel it rise and fall. Count the breaths up to five.

Body scans - Guide children to slowly tune into the body from head to toe, noticing any sensations without judging them. Release any tension or tightness.

Mindful listening - Encourage mindful listening by having children concentrate solely on sounds within and around them. Identify sounds one by one without labeling them.

. . .

Nature observation - Take children outdoors and have them use their senses to observe natural objects. Notice colors, textures, shapes, scents, and sounds non-judgmentally.

Gratitude - At bedtime or during meals, have children name things they are grateful for, such as toys, friends, family, or special moments from the day.

Loving-kindness - Help children silently extend heartfelt wishes for health and happiness toward themselves and others using mantras such as:

"May you be safe, may you be peaceful."

Mindful movement - Teach children mindful walking, yoga stretches, or slow-motion dance moves. Guide them to focus on body sensations without competition or judgment.

Sensory experiences - Provide tactile materials for children to mindfully explore, such as sand, water, clay, or fingerpaints. Encourage them to observe textures and colors closely.

Everyday activities - Incorporate mindfulness into simple routines like eating, walking, homework time, or household chores. Guide children to give full attention to each activity as they do it.

. . .

These are just some of the many techniques children can use to cultivate mindfulness as part of their daily routine. Experiment together to find out which methods your child connects with the most. The key is to make it fun rather than a chore. Just 5-10 minutes of consistent daily practice can instill powerful mindfulness skills that will benefit your child immeasurably.

CREATING A SUPPORTIVE ENVIRONMENT

For children to fully embrace mindfulness, it is vital to facilitate regular practice in an encouraging environment. Here are some tips for making mindfulness engaging:

- Set aside a consistent time each day for mindfulness, such as mornings or before bedtime. Consistency helps the practices take root.

- Guide children with a gentle, relaxed tone using simple language. Avoid criticism or judgment of their efforts.

- Start with shorter sessions of 5-10 minutes, depending on your child's age and temperament. Gradually increase over time.

- Make it interactive and fun by using games, songs, stories, nature sounds, or visual aids like glitter bottles.

- Join in and practice together. Children often learn best by observation. Demonstrate mindfulness in your own behaviors.

• Share in discussions afterward about each child's experiences. What did they notice? Did any feelings arise?

• Give children tools like journals, singing bowls, or mindfulness coloring books to foster engagement and reflection.

• Offer positive reinforcement when children demonstrate mindful behaviors without pressure for formal practice.

• Remain patient and let children progress at their own developmental pace. Moving too fast could cause resistance.

By cultivating a warm, relaxed atmosphere around mindfulness, it will become an enriching part of your child's daily routine. Children are naturally primed to learn these skills if given the right nurturing environment.

OVERCOMING POTENTIAL OBSTACLES

Introducing mindfulness to children is generally quite seamless, but you may face some typical challenges along the way:

• **Lack of motivation** - Make practices brief and engaging. Do not force children to sit still if they resist. Offer choices and give them a sense of control.

- **Limited attention span** - Start with 1-2 minutes for young children and gradually increase the time as their concentration expands. Play soft music or sounds to anchor their focus if needed.

- **Overthinking** - Remind children that mindfulness is about observing thoughts non-judgmentally, not emptying the mind. Thoughts will come and go, and that is okay.

- **Silly behavior** - Giggles and restlessness are normal. Gently guide children back to the practice without criticism. Keep the atmosphere light-hearted and fun.

- **Discouragement** - Validate that mindfulness can feel challenging at times. Emphasize that it takes practice. Remain patient and encouraging through their ups and downs.

With a compassionate, child-centered approach, you can successfully navigate these bumps along the road. Trust the process and let mindfulness blossom organically in your child's life.

Conclusion

Mindfulness is a valuable gift we can offer our children to support their growth and development. The benefits range from enhanced executive skills and emotional regulation to improved social skills, self-esteem, and resilience. While introducing new practices, remember to make it engaging and avoid pressure or strict discipline. With time and consistency using child-friendly methods, your children will flourish and thrive.

The forthcoming chapters will provide practical techniques, stories, games, and activities to seamlessly weave mindfulness into your family's daily routine. We will address common concerns and outline methods tailored for different age groups. Let us embark upon this journey together to unlock the tremendous transformative power of mindfulness for your children's well-being and your family bonds.

"THE MAGICAL FOREST"
STORYTIME:

© 2023 Manon Doucet. All rights reserved.

"The Magical Forest"

Once upon a time, in a faraway land blanketed in myth and legend, there existed an enchanted forest known as Whispering Woods. This ancient woodland was home to towering oak and maple trees, their leaves shimmering emeralds and golds. A gentle breeze danced through the forest, carrying with it ancient wisdom in soft whispers.

In this magical realm dwelled a group of woodland creatures who possessed extraordinary talents. There was Bella, a graceful doe who could outrun the wind itself. Milo, a wise old owl whose piercing night vision saw all. And Ruby, an inquisitive squirrel with a knack for uncovering nature's hidden treasures.

Together, these three creatures were guardians of the forest, protecting its magic from those who wished to exploit it. Each day, they would meet by a gently babbling brook to share news and ensure all was well in their sheltered world.

One bright sunny morning, as the friends gathered, Milo ruffled his tawny feathers uneasily.

> "My friends, I spotted something unusual while scouting last night - a young human girl wandering alone near the Whispering Willows."

Ruby's bushy tail twitched nervously.

> "A human? How worrisome. We must be sure she does not disturb the forest's delicate magic."

Just then, a snapping twig drew their attention. Whirling around, they saw a wide-eyed, red-haired girl stepping timidly into the glen.

> "Hello."

She squeaked nervously, giving a small wave.
Bella approached slowly, her footsteps feather-light.

> "Greetings, young one. What brings you to our home?"

She asked gently so as not to startle the child.
The girl's face flooded with relief at the warm welcome.

> "My name is Nerys."

She offered politely.

> "I've heard tales of the legendary Whispering Woods and wanted to experience its magic for myself."

Ruby scurried down from her perch, unable to contain her curiosity about this newcomer.

> "You've come to the right place! I'm Ruby, resident explorer extraordinaire!"

She proclaimed importantly.
Bella smiled, her liquid eyes radiating warmth.

> "And I am Bella. Welcome, Nerys."

Milo glided down soundlessly beside them.

> "I am called Milo."

He intoned, fixing Nerys with his bright yellow stare. Nerys gifted each creature a smile in return.

> "It's lovely to meet you all. I've dreamed of finding this forest ever since Gran told me the stories as a child. She said Whispering Woods holds ancient secrets that can help one find inner peace."

Nerys recounted.

The three friends exchanged knowing looks. As protectors of the forest, they sensed Nerys had a pure heart.

> "Nerys, would you like us to show you the forest's magic?"

Bella offered kindly.

At the girl's eager nod, the creatures led her deeper into the mystical woods. As Nerys walked, she trailed her hands along mossy trunks and brushed fingertips through flowers and ferns. Ruby pointed out curiosities - a deer track, a rabbit hole, a hive of droning bees.

Before long, they arrived at the heart of the forest bathed in warm sunlight - a tucked-away meadow dotted with wildflowers. Nerys drew a sharp breath, enraptured by its beauty.

> "Here we are, the whispering meadow."

Declared Ruby.

> "Our favorite spot in the whole forest."

Milo motioned with a wing to a patch of soft grass.

> "Nerys, make yourself comfortable. We want to share a special magic with you."

Settling cross-legged onto the cushiony grass, Nerys waited

expectantly. Bella and Ruby lay nearby, emanating tranquility. Milo perched on a branch above the girl's head.

> "Nerys, the true magic of Whispering Woods lies not in spells or potions but rather in the simple practice of meditation."

Nerys tilted her head curiously.

> "Meditation? But how does it work?"

Milo blinked sagely down at her.

> "It quiets the mind and soothes the spirit. Think of it as creating a peaceful oasis within yourself."

Bella nodded her elegant head.

> "It allows one to find clarity and wisdom which so often elude busy minds."

> "Will you teach me?"

Nerys implored, eyes shining with intrigue.

> "Gladly,"

replied Milo.

> "Make yourself comfortable and close your eyes. Focus on your breathing, taking long, slow breaths in and out."

As Nerys followed his guidance, Milo's hypnotic voice instructed her to clear her mind and instead picture the tranquility of the forest. Nerys envisioned verdant trees, heard birdsong and bubbling water, and smelled fragrant wildflowers. She felt her worries dissolve as the living forest filled her senses.

> "Very good,"
>
> "with regular practice, you will be able to find this inner sanctuary anytime."

Praised Milo after several serene minutes had passed.

Nerys opened her eyes, feeling peaceful yet revitalized. She turned to the guardian creatures with a smile.

> "That was wonderful! It felt like the forest was embracing me. Thank you for sharing this gift."

Ruby scampered happily around the girl.

> "Remember, you can always find your way back to this quiet grove in your mind when you need relief from the chaos of life."

Nerys committed to the memory of the meadow's sights, smells, and sounds so she could return anytime. As the sun dipped low in the sky, she knew it was time to let the creatures return to their watch.

> "I cannot thank you enough for welcoming me today and showing me the power of meditation,"

Nerys said sincerely.

> "You've given me a great treasure."

Bella and Ruby gifted her with affectionate nuzzles. Milo gazed fondly down upon her.

> "The forest has roots within you now, young one. Nurture that seed, and you will blossom."

The walk back passed swiftly as Nerys floated in a bubble of serenity. At the forest's edge, she turned with a wave.

> "Farewell, my dear friends! I hope to return soon."

> "Farewell, Nerys! May you find much peace and joy!"

Ruby called after her.

In the days that followed, whenever Nerys felt overwhelmed, she would sit quietly and mentally return to the sun-dappled glade. As she focused on her breathing, tranquility would settle over her like a warm blanket.

Before long, she ventured back to the real meadow, where Bella, Milo, and Ruby welcomed her joyfully. They were pleased to see Nerys integrating the forest's magic into her daily life.

And so Nerys became a student of the guardian creatures, visiting the meadow often to strengthen her meditation skills. In time, she even taught her family and friends this healing practice, helping them find their own inner sanctuaries.

Many years later, when old age prompted Nerys to pass down her learnings, she returned to Whispering Woods one last time. The wise old owl Milo still watched over the forest realm he loved.

Nerys lay among the whispering wildflowers, taking in the familiar sights and sounds.

> "Thank you, dear friend."

She whispered,

> "for what you have given me - a lifetime of peace."

As she breathed her last, a gentle breeze swirled through the glade...and distantly, drifted the sound of owl wings, escorting Nerys' spirit into the next life.

The End

CHAPTER 3
TEACHING CHILDREN EFFECTIVE COMMUNICATION
EMPOWERING CHILDREN THROUGH EFFECTIVE COMMUNICATION

TEACHING EMOTIONAL AWARENESS AND REGULATION

A CHILD'S emotional landscape is complex and ever-evolving. As they grow and develop, children experience a diverse range of emotions, from joy to anger, excitement to disappointment. Learning to navigate this emotional terrain is essential for their overall well-being and success.

In this chapter, we provide parents and caregivers with practical guidance on nurturing emotional awareness and regulation skills in children. We explore age-appropriate strategies for identifying emotions, modeling healthy responses, teaching coping mechanisms, and fostering resilience. Our aim is to equip you with actionable tools to help children master their emotions rather than be mastered by them.

THE VALUE OF EMOTIONAL AWARENESS AND REGULATION

> "Emotions drive learning, decision-making, creativity, relationships, and health. Developing the skills to handle emotions well is especially important for children," observes neuroscientist Dr. Daniel Goleman, author of Emotional Intelligence (Goleman, 2006).

Beyond cognition, a child's ability to recognize, express, and regulate their emotions in constructive ways is essential for navigating life's challenges.

> Research shows that challenges like anxiety, aggression, and depression in children are closely linked to difficulties with emotional self-regulation (Newman & Newman, 2017).

> Conversely, kids who demonstrate strong emotional awareness and management exhibit greater self-control, confidence, and empathy and report a higher life satisfaction. (Medicine et al., 2016)

The capacity to handle emotions adaptively relies heavily on the development of neural connections between the amygdala and the prefrontal cortex. The amygdala acts as the brain's emotional center, while the prefrontal cortex governs executive functions like planning, focus, and impulse control.

"Activities that strengthen connections between these two areas lead to greater emotional intelligence," explains Dr. Uma Naidoo, author of This Is Your Brain on Food (Naidoo, 2020).

Teaching children to identify and respond to emotions thoughtfully helps guide the brain's wiring in positive directions. These neural networks form the basis for skills like resilience, relationship-building, and decision-making, which are critical for mental health and success.

By nurturing emotional awareness and regulation early in childhood, parents and caregivers provide a valuable foundation that supports children across their lifespan.

FOSTERING EMOTIONAL AWARENESS

Developing emotional awareness starts with being able to recognize and label different feelings. Children absorb many emotional cues from observing those around them. Caregivers can explicitly name emotions as they arise:

> "I can see the big smile on your face. You look really happy now that we're going to the park."

> "When your sister took your toy, you got very angry. It's okay to feel angry sometimes."

> "I know you're disappointed that your friend couldn't come over. It's hard when our plans change unexpectedly."

Using feeling words in everyday conversations, books, songs, and games exposes children to a nuanced emotional vocabulary. The wider the range of feeling words they can connect to internal states, the greater their self-awareness.

In addition to labeling emotions, guide children to identify how emotions manifest physically within their bodies. For example, when angry, they may experience clenched fists or a tensed jaw. When scared, they may notice a rapid heartbeat or trembling hands. Tuning into these bodily cues builds their mind-body awareness.

Promoting self-reflection is another path to expanding emotional awareness. Children can benefit from gentle prompts like:

> "How did you feel when your brother broke your toy?"

> "What happened today that made you feel proud?"

> "What do you do when you feel nervous before a test?"

Open-ended questions encourage children to reflect inward rather than simply react to external events. Listening attentively and non-judgmentally to their responses validates the importance of inner experiences.

Over time, consistent modeling and interactive discussion around emotions enhances children's vocabulary, mind-body connection, and introspective ability. This self-awareness empowers them to better understand their own responses and behaviors.

TEACHING HEALTHY EMOTIONAL RESPONSES

> Once children can identify emotions, caregivers play a key role in teaching adaptive ways of responding. Dr. Daniel Siegel, clinical professor of psychiatry at UCLA School of Medicine, offers this guidance:
>
> "When a child has a feeling, the goal is not to try to stop it but to help the child learn to regulate and channel it in useful ways. Responding with empathy validates their inner experience and models healthy coping." (Siegel, 2015)

Dismissing, denying, or punishing children's emotions communicates that their feelings are wrong or unacceptable. This causes children to suppress feelings rather than process them.

On the other hand, a compassionate response shows children they can safely share vulnerable emotions. This lays the groundwork for managing negative feelings constructively rather than being paralyzed by them.

. . .

When responding to challenging behaviors stemming from intense emotions, avoid criticism of the feeling itself. Rather, re-direct the energy behind it. For example, if a child hits others in anger, you might say,

> "I know you feel like hitting when you're angry. Let's go take some deep breaths or walk to cool down instead."

This acknowledges the emotion while guiding toward a more positive expression.

Children also learn by observing adult role models. Caregivers can narrate their own process of working through difficult feelings:

> "When I feel overwhelmed, taking some deep breaths helps me calm down and think clearly again."

> "I can see you're really frustrated. I get frustrated, too, sometimes. Let me show you how I use my pillow to punch safely until I feel better."

> "I'm feeling a bit sad today remembering Grandpa. Let's look at our photo album together and talk about the happy memories."

By vocalizing their emotional coping strategies, adults provide children with concrete examples of healthy self-regulation.

TEACHING COPING SKILLS

Equipping children with specific techniques for coping with intense emotions is essential for their ability to self-regulate. Particularly during early childhood, caregivers act as external regulators, guiding children to use adaptive tools independently over time. Helpful coping skills to teach include:

Deep breathing:

Teach children to take slow, full breaths to stimulate the parasympathetic nervous system and promote relaxation. Using visuals like blowing bubbles or a balloon can help. Practice when they are calm so it becomes a familiar coping strategy.

Muscle relaxation:

Progressive muscle relaxation involves tensing and relaxing muscle groups one by one. Tightening and releasing the muscles alleviates tension and anxiety. Lead children through the sequence using games and imagery.

Talking it through:

Encourage children to verbalize their feelings and what led to them. Putting emotions into words develops cognitive control and minimizes rumination. Be an active listener without immediately proposing solutions.

Physical outlets:

Provide safe physical outlets like pillow punching, ripping paper, clay sculpting, or using a punching bag. These release pent-up energy associated with emotions like anger, frustration, or anxiety.

. . .

Mindfulness:

Teach children to pause and observe their inner experiences without judgment. Mindful breathing, body scans, and visualization can induce calm in heated moments by activating the prefrontal cortex.

Creative expression:

Expressive outlets like drawing, painting, dancing, singing, or writing allow children to release emotions through creation rather than destruction. Identifying patterns in their creative expressions also builds self-awareness.

Humor:

In appropriate contexts, humor can lighten the mood and put feelings into perspective. Funny movies, jokes, or silly interactions remind children not to take themselves too seriously. Laughter produces endorphins that reduce stress chemicals.

Social support:

Encourage children to seek support from trusted others to share their feelings. This might include talking to parents, writing in a journal, playing with friends, or spending time with a pet. Supportive connections comfort and replenish them.

Positive self-talk:

Teach children to use affirmative self-talk to counter negative thinking and self-criticism. Statements like

> "I can handle this."

"This feeling will pass."

"I am strong."

or

"Mistakes help me improve."

Cultivate optimism.

Using these methods consistently over time equips children with a toolbox of coping skills they can utilize independently when faced with emotional overwhelm.

BUILDING RESILIENCE THROUGH PLAY

The wonder of imaginative play gives children a forum to creatively explore their inner landscape. As Fred Rogers wisely said,

> "Play is really the work of childhood. It's very purposeful. It helps children learn to regulate their feelings and behavior." (Bratton & Landreth, 2019)

Play enables children to:
- Express feelings in a safe, non-threatening way.
- Experiment with different emotional responses.
- Practice regulating emotions.

. . .

Additionally, play builds confidence, adaptability, problem-solving, and executive functioning—all skills that underpin resilience.

To leverage the power of play:

Allow free play: Instead of structuring playtime, let child-led imagination and exploration unfold organically. This enables authentic emotional expression and self-directed learning.

Use props: Provide toys, dress-ups, art supplies, and building materials to spur creative scenarios. Props give shape to inner concepts.

Be a play partner: Join children in play without directing plots. By mirroring their tone and actions, you provide compassionate companionship in their emotional journey.

Allow resolutions: Avoid intervening quickly to redirect play if emotions intensify. Let scenes run their course as children imaginatively grapple with feelings.

Ask open questions: Gently discuss children's emotions during and after playtime. Ask about their feelings regarding different story events without judgment.

. . .

When children engage in play devoid of adult criticism and control, it provides a sanctuary for them to safely encounter difficult emotions. They experiment with roles, act out vulnerabilities, and organically develop coping skills. Play cultivates resilience by instilling self-efficacy and emotional adaptability.

AGE-SPECIFIC STRATEGIES

The development of emotional intelligence follows a progressive arc as children's capacities evolve. Understanding emotional milestones provides a guide for realistic expectations and tailored guidance.

INFANCY (0 -1 YEAR):

- Babies begin recognizing and responding to caregiver emotions through facial expressions and tone of voice. Frequent face-to-face interaction builds foundational emotional awareness.

- Comfort infants when distressed by meeting basic needs, soothing through touch, and maintaining a calm presence. This teaches them that emotions are manageable.

- Mirror and validate emotional expressions verbally and through mimicking sounds and gestures. This helps infants integrate emotions and behavior.

TODDLERHOOD (1-3 YEARS):

- Identify and label emotions toddlers are experiencing. Use simple feeling words in books, games, and conversations to build emotional understanding.

- With guidance and repetition, teach toddlers simple coping skills like breathing, dancing to music, or hugging a teddy when upset. This lays the groundwork for self-regulation.

- Allow toddlers to express feelings through tantrums safely. Stay present and patiently reorient their energy toward constructive outlets like play or reading a book.

- Model identifying your own feelings and appropriate responses. Narrate your process of calming yourself when angry or seeking alone time when overwhelmed.

PRESCHOOL (3-5 YEARS):

- Encourage children to identify emotional causes and consequences. Ask questions like

> "How did you feel when your friend grabbed your toy?"

To build causal links.

. . .

- Teach coping skills like talking feelings through, using art and play for expression, breathing exercises, or seeking support when distressed.

- Practice recognizing nonverbal cues like facial expressions, gestures, and tone of voice that indicate emotions. Linking these to feeling words develops emotional perception.

- Validate ALL feelings, helping children differentiate between emotions and actions. Explain that all feelings are okay, but some behaviors may be inappropriate.

- Allow child-led cooperative play to encourage negotiating emotions and conflicts, sharing, and developing empathy.

SCHOOL-AGE (6-12 YEARS):

- Engage children in conversations around managing challenging emotions like embarrassment, anxiety, sadness, or defensiveness.

- Help children reframe unhelpful thoughts and self-talk using positive affirmations to build resilience.

- Encourage journaling, art, or discussion to reflect on feelings and relieve emotional pressure. Foster positive coping habits.

- Expand emotional vocabulary by reading books or watching shows that portray more complex feelings like hopelessness, grief, or inadequacy. Discuss these emotions and how to respond healthily.

- Teach relaxation techniques like guided imagery, deep breathing, or progressive muscle relaxation to reduce stress and strong emotions.

   - Allow creative expression through music, theater, writing, dance, or sports that enable emotional release and build confidence.

The strategies above offer age-specific guidance while recognizing individual differences in the pace of emotional development. By tailoring your approach to your child's unique needs and abilities, you can provide sensitive support for their ongoing growth.

CREATING A COMPASSIONATE ENVIRONMENT

For children to truly develop emotional skills, they need an open, understanding environment. The following elements contribute to a compassionate home atmosphere:

Active listening – Give full attention when children express emotions. Avoid interrupting or problem-solving immediately. Let them convey their inner experience.

Unconditional warmth – Ensure children feel loved regardless of their emotions. Do not withdraw affection as a consequence of negative feelings. What feels intolerable is the feeling, not the child.

Emotional validation – Avoid criticizing, shaming, or punishing children for their emotions. Acknowledge the feeling and, if needed, gently re-direct behavior. Make sure they know all emotions are acceptable.

Autonomy support – Allow children to make developmentally appropriate choices over matters like food, play, friends, and interests. Nurture their sense of inner wisdom by respecting their preferences.

Relational time – Prioritize regular one-on-one time focused fully on the child. Meaningful interactions foster trust and meet their need for attention and connection.

Modeling vulnerability – Let children see your own struggles, tears, apologies, and efforts to handle emotions constructively. Your openness gives them permission to share freely without feeling flawed.

Reframing challenges – When children struggle with strong emotions, frame it as an opportunity to learn rather than a punishment or failure. Emphasize effort over perfection.

. . .

Outlets for expression – Provide creative avenues for safely expressing emotions like play, art, music, or physical exertion. Support healthy catharsis.

Empathy building – Foster compassion by discussing others' feelings in stories and real life. Ask children how they would feel if they were in someone else's situation.

By cultivating a home environment founded on compassion and understanding, parents provide fertile ground for children's emotional skills to flourish.

COMMON CONCERNS

As you guide children in developing emotional awareness and regulation, some common concerns may arise:

My child has frequent intense emotional outbursts and tantrums. Remain calm and present. Once escalated, logic cannot penetrate emotional chaos. After the storm passes, empathize and explore what triggered such distress. Also, evaluate if stressors need to be adjusted.

When I validate my child's feelings, it seems to reinforce their tantrums. Ensure your validation does not extend to unacceptable behavior. Affirm the emotion itself while setting limits on aggression. Sink below the behavior to address the root feelings.

. . .

My child struggles to verbalize their emotions and shuts down when upset. Don't force them to talk but stay nearby offering silent support through the upset. Then revisit the situation later by asking what they imagine you felt during the incident. This indirectly accesses their perspective.

I feel guilty disciplining my child when I should be compassionate. Healthy parenting involves both compassion and necessary limits. However, consequences should relate logically to the behavior, not the emotion itself. Explain this distinction clearly.

I struggle with my own emotional regulation. How can I teach these skills? Honestly, acknowledging your challenges makes you more relatable. Explain how you use strategies like pausing, breathing, or seeking help when emotions feel too big. Model being a learner.

My child seems unwilling to discuss or express emotions. First, ensure your responses are consistently empathetic. Then express confidence in your child's inner strength to handle feelings that may feel uncomfortable. Patience and creativity are key for reluctant sharers.

Remember, every child travels at their own pace in developing these complex skills. By offering consistent empathy, modeling vulnerability, teaching coping skills, allowing creativity, and framing setbacks positively, their capacities will organically blossom over time. Progress may not always be linear, but your compassion provides sustaining shelter.

Conclusion

In a culture that praises stoicism over emotional competence, parents play a vital role in cultivating skills like self-awareness, healthy expression, resilience, and empathy in children. These capacities serve as lifelong tools enabling adaptive responses to stress, strong decision-making, fulfilling relationships, and overall well-being.

While teaching emotional intelligence requires dedication and sensitivity to each child's needs, the long-term rewards are immeasurable. By guiding children to embrace all feelings with wisdom and compassion, we empower them to navigate their inner worlds with confidence, clarity, and courage—peerless skills that unlock their highest potential. Our compassion plants seeds that blossom for generations to come.

"THE EMOTION EXPRESS"
STORYTIME:

© 2023 Foss Plus. All rights reserved.

THE AMAZING JOURNEY OF LAURIE AND THE EMOTION EXPRESS

Laurie took a deep, steadying breath as she stood on the bustling platform, suitcase in hand. This was it - the start of her long-anticipated voyage aboard the mystical Emotion Express. She soaked in the sights and sounded around her - billowing clouds of steam hissing from the mighty engine, the grind of gears and the chalky scent of coal, and the melodic chimes signaling all aboard.

Laurie turned to wave one last goodbye to her family, their faces beaming with pride and anticipation. Then, with excited butterflies fluttering in her stomach, she made her way toward the gleaming train cars lined up ahead.

Each car shimmered in a different vibrant hue - crimson, sapphire, emerald, and amber. Laurie chose the emerald car and hefted her suitcase up the stairs, where she was welcomed warmly by the conductor, Jones. His crisp navy uniform complemented his jolly smile.

> "Welcome aboard, Laurie! We're thrilled you'll be joining us on this extraordinary inner journey. Let me show you to your private cabin."

Laurie followed Jones down the plushly carpeted hallway, admiring the intricate woodwork and engraved glass of each cabin door they passed. At the rear of the car, he slid open a polished door to reveal her cozy accommodations - complete with a panoramic window overlooking the receding platform.

Laurie sank into the cushioned bench by the window, waving one last time to her family as the train lurched forward. Picking up speed, the Emotion Express chugged out of the station toward the first stop on its mystical route - the Land of Joy.

Laurie watched eagerly as the urban landscape melted into rolling green hills dotted with wildflowers. The faint scent of honeysuckle drifted in through the cracked window as the train began to slow.

When it coasted to a stop amidst sunny meadows swaying with golden grain, Laurie hurried to disembark. There she was greeted by her joy guide, Bella, whose springy curls and broad smile radiated contagious enthusiasm.

> "Welcome to the Land of Joy!"

Bella cheered, enveloping Laurie in a quick hug.

> "I just know we'll have an absolutely delightful time together."

She led Laurie down a winding path through fields of fragrant daffodils, their yellow heads bobbing in the warm breeze. The floral sweetness mingled with grassy undertones, creating a scent of pure joy.

Finding a sunny clearing, Bella plopped onto the soft grass and motioned for Laurie to do the same.

> "Now, let's try a laughter meditation together."

Sitting cross-legged, they began taking deep belly breaths in unison. On each exhale, Bella let out a series of silly giggles, urging Laurie to join in. Soon, they were both collapsing into fits of contagious laughter for no reason besides the pure delight of it.

With each round of mirth, Laurie could feel joy bubbling up from deep within her core, leaving her cheeks flushed and eyes sparkling with levity. She had never felt so carefree and lighter than air.

After several blissful minutes, Bella handed Laurie a vibrant yellow sunflower.

> "Here's a little memento of the Land of Joy. Remember, you can access this feeling anytime with mindfulness and an open heart."

Laurie inhaled the sunflower's sweet, earthy aroma, imprinting this moment of joy. As she boarded the Emotion Express once more, she blew Bella a kiss, eager for what lay ahead.

The train chugged on through emerald hills before arriving at snowcapped mountains - the Land of Calm. Laurie's excitement grew as the frosty air nipped at her cheeks while disembarking.

Her guide, Sage, greeted Laurie with a bow, his voice as steady as the mountains around them.

> "Welcome. I'm Sage, and I'll be your calmness guide today."

His saffron robe fluttered gently in the mountain breeze.

He led Laurie along a winding stone path to an ancient garden nestled between the soaring peaks. A babbling brook provided the only sound breaking the profound stillness.

Finding a smooth boulder beneath a cherry tree, Sage guided Laurie into a meditative breathing exercise.

> "Focus on each inhalation and exhalation."

He intoned, voice resonating with tranquility.

As Laurie followed his instructions, the sweet scent of blossoms filled her senses. With each cycle of breath, she felt layers of tension melt away, leaving behind profound serenity.

When the meditation concluded, Sage presented Laurie with a polished stone.

> "A reminder of the calm you discovered today.
> Carry it with you always."

Boarding the train once more, Laurie caressed the smooth surface of the stone, its energy already infusing her with tranquility.

The Emotion Express chugged on through the mountains into a new landscape - the fiery Land of Anger. Jagged cliffs towered above, and distant rumblings echoed warnings of simmering rage.

Kenta, Laurie's warrior guide, met her on the platform with a stern nod.

> "Welcome. Anger can be harnessed into productive energy if expressed properly."

He led Laurie along a path between looming cliffs to a valley of steam vents and bubbling lava pools.

> "This is a place for safe release. Follow my lead."

Kenta demonstrated a series of punches and kicks, accentuating each with a fierce shout.

Laurie mirrored his movements, feeling absurd at first. But with each yell, she felt sparks of buried frustrations surface, flowing out through her fists and feet. Soon she was punching with purpose, converted anger morphing into righteous indignation.

By the end, Laurie panted with exertion but felt oddly cleansed. Kenta handed her a crimson stone.

> "Well done. Remember, anger can strengthen resolve if channeled constructively."

Boarding the train, Laurie studied the red stone's flickering depths, understanding anger's potential for positive change.

The Emotion Express delivered Laurie next to the bittersweet Land of Sadness. Stepping onto the platform, she was engulfed by an aura of melancholy - weeping willows swaying over a placid lagoon.

Tiana, Laurie's empathetic guide, took her hand gently.

> "This place honors sorrow. Let's reflect on how sadness connects us."

Seated beneath the trailing willow branches, Tiana led Laurie through a loving-kindness meditation.

> "Visualize those burdened with grief. Send them compassion."

Laurie focused on radiating warmth to lonely, hurting souls. Soon, tears spilled down her cheeks. With Tiana's guidance, she redirected the compassion inward, embracing her own sorrows with self-love.

The experience left Laurie feeling solemn yet cleansed. Tiana gifted her a teardrop-shaped pendant.

> "A symbol of sadness transmuted into wisdom and love."

As the Emotion Express pulled away once more, Laurie fingered the pendant thoughtfully. She could now appreciate sorrow's gift of profound empathy.

At last, Laurie's epic journey delivered her back home to the bustling station she had left just days before. Yet she herself had changed. Each realm unlocked wisdom and nuance about the nature of human emotions.

Laurie's family awaited on the platform, their eyes shining with joyful tears. As Laurie rushed into their embrace, she saw that though she had ventured far, the true destination had been within her all along.

From that day forward, she embraced her emotional landscape in its full complexity - its joy and calm, anger and sadness. Just as the Emotion Express had connected diverse realms, Laurie now saw herself as one whole, with each feeling playing its part.

The End

CHAPTER 4
4 CULTIVATING INNER PEACE TO RESOLVE OUTER CONFLICT
CULTIVATING INNER PEACE TO RESOLVE OUTER CONFLICT

> "In the midst of chaos, there is also opportunity."
> • Sun Tzu

CONFLICT MANIFESTS TURBULENCE in children's lives, stirring up emotions like frustration, anger, and hurt. While disagreements often appear chaotic on the surface, they present profound opportunities to cultivate understanding, empathy, and relationship-strengthening problem-solving skills.

By introducing children to meditation, we equip them with an invaluable toolkit to transform conflict into an enlightening journey of growth. Meditation grants children the inner stillness to approach disagreements with wisdom, convert chaos into calm, and discover shared solutions through empathy.

. . .

This chapter illuminates practical ways caregivers can guide children to draw upon meditation amidst conflicts with siblings, friends, teachers, and peers. Integrating mindfulness into children's lives lays the foundation of emotional awareness, self-regulation, compassionate communication, and creative conflict resolution. With these tools, children gain the insight to convert outer conflicts into inner peace.

UNDERSTANDING CONFLICT'S ROOT CAUSES

The starting point in nurturing harmonious conflict resolution skills is examining the nature of conflict itself. Conflict arises when needs, desires, or perspectives clash. Share examples of everyday conflicts - two siblings arguing over a toy, classmates disagreeing about the rules of a game, wanting to play different activities.

Highlight that disagreements and arguments are a natural occurrence within human relationships, even loving families and close friendships. Tension does not necessarily signify a flawed relationship but rather two valid but differing viewpoints.

Explain that each conflict contains seeds of understanding and growth. The goal is not to label winners and losers but to find solutions that work for both parties. With empathy, mindfulness, and problem-solving skills, children can learn to resolve disagreements constructively, even strengthening their relationships in the process.

Use stories, role-plays, and real-life examples to expand children's insight into common triggers that spark conflict:

- **Competing needs and desires** - Both children want the same toy.
- **Differing communication styles** - One child prefers noisy play, while the other likes quiet activities.
- **Misunderstandings** - A child misreads a classmate's joke as unfriendly.
- **Struggles over resources** - Two children both want to use the same space.
- **Strong emotions** - A child feels jealous when friends play without him.
- **Differing values and opinions** - Friends argue over what game to play.

By fostering awareness of these common catalysts, children gain the discernment to better identify sources of disagreement at the moment instead of being carried away by reactivity.

MANAGING STRONG EMOTIONS WITH MINDFULNESS

In the heat of conflict, children often experience intense surges of anger, frustration, hurt, or anxiety. These strong emotions can overwhelm logic and impede conflict resolution. Children require guidance to manage difficult feelings effectively.

Introduce children to mindfulness practices that help calm emotional storms by bringing attention to the present moment. Simple breathing exercises teach children to pause and gain perspective instead of feeding conflict through impulsive reactions.

· · ·

Have children sit comfortably. Place one hand on the belly and one on the chest. Instruct them to inhale slowly through the nose, feeling the belly expand with the breath. Exhale gently through the mouth. Repeat for a few minutes until breathing settles into an even, smooth rhythm. This calms the nervous system.

Teach children to notice physical cues when upset - tensed shoulders, clenched jaw, knotted stomach. Have them stop and take a few deep breaths until the body relaxes. This builds awareness of their own stress signals.

Guide children to pay attention to the feet pressing into the floor sounds in the room, and sensations of clothing on the skin. These exercises ground children in the present, limiting the spiral into distress. Even one mindful minute can help diffuse emotional buildup.

Validate children's difficulties in regulating emotions. With compassion, encourage the use of healthy coping strategies like talking to trusted adults, writing in a journal, or discharging energy through safe physical activities. Emotional awareness and self-soothing skills are lifelong tools for navigating disputes calmly.

COMMUNICATING NEEDS WITH MINDFUL CLARITY

As emotions settle through mindfulness, children become equipped to express their own needs and listen to others with empathy - the building blocks of conflict resolution.

. . .

Explain common communication roadblocks that spark disputes - blaming statements, disrespectful language, interrupting, ignoring perspectives, and yelling. Role-play examples followed by more mindful reframes:

Less mindful:

> "You always take my toys without asking. You are so selfish!"

More mindful:

> "When you borrow my toys without my permission, I feel frustrated because I was still using them. In the future, please ask before taking my belongings."

Less mindful:

> "I don't care if you were here first; move over! I want to sit there."

More mindful:

> "I understand you were sitting there first. I would like to sit in that spot too. Is there a way we could take turns or find another solution?"

Guide children to express themselves using **"I"** statements rather than accusations. Encourage respectful language even in disagreement. Explore how volume and tone impact outcomes. These exercises equip children with the nuanced communication capacities to resolve conflict.

Along with speaking mindfully, teach the art of listening deeply. When listening to another's perspective, have children maintain eye contact, paraphrase what was said, and ask thoughtful questions to gain clarity. Role-play active listening using age-appropriate conflicts as examples.

COMPASSION, THE CORNERSTONE OF CONFLICT RESOLUTION

Empathy constitutes the core of harmonious conflict resolution. Children's abilities to step into others' shoes and understand their positions expand the field of solutions.

We cultivate empathy in children through mindfulness meditation. Have children sit comfortably and close their eyes. Guide them to visualize scenarios from different perspectives:

Imagine feeling left out when your best friends play together without you. What emotions arise? Now imagine you just made a new friend who feels left out. What could you do to help them feel included?

Visualize wanting to use your new art set, but your sibling is playing with it. How does your body feel? Now imagine you are the sibling who wants to finish what you are building. What solutions might meet both needs?

Use characters from books and stories as examples to contemplate different positions. What was the scout's viewpoint when her troop excluded her? Why did the king make rules the villagers disagreed with? Literature provides abundant opportunities to grow empathy.

. . .

When disagreements do arise, take a minute to breathe together. Then have each child share their perspective and needs, really listening to understand the other. Compassionate listening uncovers solutions hidden beneath the conflict's surface.

Guide children to identify areas of common ground during disputes. Do you both value fairness? Want to maintain the friendship? This builds the foundation of mutual understanding and creative problem-solving.

RESOLVING CONFLICTS COLLABORATIVELY

Once children learn to calm inner storms and connect with compassion, they are equipped to collaboratively solve interpersonal conflicts through shared dialogue.

Teach a simple framework using the acronym OPTIONS:
- Open dialogue with "I" statements.

> "I feel concerned when I'm left out of games."

- Perspectives. Listen to understand all viewpoints.

> "I see you wanted alone time with Jessie."

- Tensions. Identify the key tensions or triggers.

> "We both want to play with the same toys right now."

- Innovations. Brainstorm creative solutions.

> "Take turns using the art set for 15 minutes each?"

- Options. Discuss options that meet mutual needs.

> "Or use different sections of the playroom?"

- Negotiate agreement.

> "Let's take turns today and tomorrow to create a schedule."

- Solutions. Implement compromises and revisit as needed.

> "This works better now that we have a plan."

Have children practice walking through the OPTIONS model using age-appropriate scenarios - two kids arguing over a ball at recess, siblings disputing the use of a video game, etc. With guided practice, this framework becomes second nature.

Remind children that conflict resolution is about creating mutual understanding - identifying shared goals, and generating win-win compromises. Differences will continue to arise, but mindfulness grants the capacity to face them with empathy and wisdom.

INTEGRATING MINDFULNESS INTO DAILY LIFE

For children to effectively bring mindfulness to conflict, caregivers must nurture its practice in daily life, not just during disputes. Set a peaceful tone through mindful role modeling.

· · ·

Start family meals with a moment of gratitude or loving-kindness meditation. Share your own mindful pauses - the deep breath before a difficult call, a restorative walk after an argument with a partner. Describe how mindfulness centers your emotional responses.

Incorporate mindfulness into the family routine - listening to chimes or a soothing song to transition from playtime to bedtime, a tech-free quiet hour after school, and breathing exercises to unwind difficult emotions.

Watch for everyday opportunities to guide children to pause and tune into sensations, sounds, or visions of beauty around them - a flower's perfume, sunlight sparkling on the water, the rhythm of their steps. Integrating these reminders builds mindfulness muscle memory.

Most importantly, meet conflict with gentle compassion, both for the child and oneself. Emotional outbursts signal a need for connection and coaching. Respond with empathy, then revisit the situation when everyone is calm. Each conflict presents a learning opportunity.

By nurturing the soil of mindfulness, we create an environment where children's inner resources can take root and blossom into wisdom. With time and guidance, they gain the insight to transform life's inevitable conflicts into opportunities for understanding - watering the seeds of empathy and peace.

"THE PLAYGROUND PROBLEM SOLVERS"
STORYTIME:

© 2023 Manon Doucet. All rights reserved.

"The Playground Problem Solvers"

It was a sunny spring morning at Sunnyville Elementary School. Students of all ages flooded onto the playground for recess, eager to soak up the warm rays and enjoy the fresh air after sitting in stuffy classrooms.

Among them was Nancy, a bright-eyed girl with curly blonde hair framing her cheerful face. Humming a playful tune, she found an empty spot on the blacktop and knelt down with a piece of chalk in hand. Tongue poking out in concentration, Nancy began drawing a meticulous hopscotch board, carefully lining up each numbered square.

Nancy became fully engrossed in her task, appreciating the satisfying squeak of the chalk against the pavement. In her mind, she was designing the perfect game for her and her friends to enjoy. Each line had to be straight and even for optimal gameplay.

After double-checking her work, Nancy stood back with her hands on her hips, admiring the completed board with pride. She couldn't wait to gather her friends and explain the rules for her new hopscotch creation!

Just then, a blur of motion in the corner of her eye made Nancy turn her head sharply. Derek came barreling across the blacktop, focused intently on dribbling a soccer ball. His eyes were glued to the ball, oblivious to his surroundings.

Before Nancy could shout a warning, Derek's shoe scuffed right through her meticulous chalk grid, smudging the numbers and lines into an illegible mess.

"Hey!"

Nancy cried out, her initial delight morphing into frustration. All her hard work was ruined! She fought to reign in her spiking anger, remembering the mindfulness tips her mom had taught her.

Closing her eyes, Nancy focused on taking a few deep, calming breaths. As the oxygen circulated through her body, she felt her tensed shoulders relax and her furrowed brow smooth out.

Opening her eyes, Nancy turned to Derek, who was staring at the chalky smears looking perplexed.

> "Oh geez, did I do that?"

he asked.

> "I'm really sorry, Nancy! I was so focused on my ball that I didn't even see your game."

Pride swelled in Nancy's chest. Her mindfulness technique had worked! Instead of snapping, she found compassion for her friend, who had made an honest mistake.

> "It's okay, Derek."

she replied.

> "I know you didn't mean it. But I did work really hard on that hopscotch design. Do you think you could help me redraw the parts you smudged?"

Derek's face flooded with relief.

> "Of course!"

he agreed.

> "It was an accident, but I should still help fix it. That's what friends do."

Nancy handed him a piece of chalk, touched by his willingness to make amends. Together, they repaired the damaged sections, carefully rewriting the numbers and straightening each line.

As they worked, Nancy appreciated the unexpected gift of getting to collaborate with her friend. She made a mental note to communicate mindfully whenever problems popped up in the future.

Just as she and Derek were finishing up, Nancy noticed another classmate named Luis sitting glumly nearby. His drooped shoulders and glum expression signaled something was wrong.

Nancy wandered over and sat down next to him.

> "What's going on, Luis? You seem really upset about something.

She said, keeping her voice gentle and concerned.

Luis gestured to the basketball court where some rowdy older kids were playing a raucous game of three-on-three.

> "Them!"

He huffed angrily. "I asked Jamal if I could join their game, and he said I'm too little and would mess it up."

Nancy nodded in understanding, though inwardly, she felt a swell of injustice on her friend's behalf. No one deserved to be left out or put down.

> "I'm really sorry to hear that, Luis."

She offered sincerely. Then an idea sprang to mind.

> "I bet if I go talk to Jamal calmly, he'll change his mind. Want me to give it a try?"

> "You'd do that for me?"

Luis asked, eyes wide with surprise and appreciation. At Nancy's enthusiastic nod, he broke into a grin.

> "That would be awesome! You're the best."

Bolstered by her success with Derek, Nancy strode confidently onto the basketball court and waved to get Jamal's attention. When he jogged over to her, she kept her voice friendly but firm.

> "Hi, Jamal! I know you're trying to keep your game competitive, but Luis is feeling really left out. I think it would mean a lot to him if you let him join in, even just for one round. What do you say?"

Jamal glanced uncertainly over at Luis, who was watching this exchange with bated breath. After a moment's consideration, Jamal nodded.

> "You're right; that was pretty mean of me,"

he admitted.

> "This court is for everyone."

He waved Luis over.

> "Hey, sorry about that, Luis. Come join my team!"

Luis's crestfallen face morphed into one of astonished delight.

> "Really? You mean it?"

At Jamal's assurance, Luis whooped and raced onto the court, giving Nancy an exuberant high-five along the way.

Nancy beamed proudly as she watched Luis joyfully join the action. Thanks to clear communication and empathy, she transformed an exclusionary situation into one of inclusion and justice.

As she headed back to her hopscotch board, Nancy marveled at the power she held to solve playground problems with compassion. She realized that by speaking up respectfully and elevating the needs of others, she could spread more light in the world, even if just within the fences of Sunnyville School.

From that day on, Nancy embraced her role as a playground peacemaker. Whenever disputes or hurt feelings arose, she listened generously and offered thoughtful solutions. Her patience and willingness to understand both sides of a disagreement made her a trusted friend and mediator.

And for Nancy, few feelings could compare to the satisfaction of turning would-be conflicts into new opportunities for friendship. She had discovered that with caring communication, playground squabbles never had to turn into playground tears.

The End.

CHAPTER 5
CULTIVATING RESILIENCE AND SELF-REGULATION IN CHILDREN THROUGH MINDFULNESS

IN OUR COMPLEX and fast-paced world, children face increasing pressures from school, social dynamics, technology, and growing up. These stressors can manifest in emotional reactivity, impulsiveness, anxiety, and difficulty coping with life's inevitable challenges. However, the good news is mindfulness offers parents a powerful tool to strengthen resilience and self-regulation skills in children.

In this chapter, we provide practical guidance and scientifically-backed research on how mindfulness bolsters resilience, improves self-control, enhances focus, and empowers adaptive coping. Our aim is to equip parents and caregivers with practical tools to nurture these crucial life skills in children through mindfulness techniques tailored for their developmental stage.

WHY RESILIENCE MATTERS

Resilience is defined as the ability to navigate life's inevitable difficulties and setbacks with flexibility, optimism, and emotional stability.

> Numerous studies demonstrate that resilient children have greater academic achievement, mental well-being, and social competence compared to their less resilient peers ((Gullotta & Adams, 2007).

Neuroscience reveals that resilience relies heavily on executive functioning skills governed by the prefrontal cortex of the brain. These include cognitive flexibility, emotional regulation, planning, and impulse control.

> "Mindfulness strengthens the prefrontal cortex and the brain's executive functioning capacity, which are the neurological underpinnings of resilience," explains neuropsychologist (Medicine et al., 2019)

For parents, nurturing resilience provides children with an inner toolkit of adaptability and grit to handle adversity. Resilient kids are able to shift perspectives, regulate their emotions, and demonstrate perseverance when faced with obstacles. These skills enable them to approach challenges as opportunities for growth rather than threats.

. . .

Mindfulness is a powerful way parents can cultivate resilience skills from a young age, providing children with protective life armor. The key is tailoring mindfulness practices to their developmental stage and making them consistent.

SELF-REGULATION: A CORNERSTONE OF RESILIENCE

Closely tied to resilience is a child's capacity for self regulation the ability to consciously guide one's thoughts, emotions, and behaviors. This involves skills like controlling impulses, focusing attention, and adapting to situational demands.

> "Self-regulation relies heavily on executive functioning in areas like the prefrontal cortex and anterior cingulate cortex that govern self-control. Mindfulness meditation has been shown to increase activity and gray matter density in these brain regions and improve self-regulation," explains a neuroscientist (Tang, 2017).

Children with stronger self-regulation exhibit greater social competence, academic performance, and ability to handle stressful situations. Poor self-regulation is linked to challenges like ADHD, aggression, anxiety, and depression (Murray et al., 2015). Helping children hone their self-control abilities provides lifelong benefits.

Mindfulness is a foundational practice for developing self-mastery. By repeatedly bringing their attention to the present moment, children train their minds to stay focused and composed. Gradually, self-regulation becomes an ingrained habit rather than a struggle.

INFUSING MINDFULNESS INTO DAILY LIFE

Mindfulness is most effective when children practice regularly for short periods, such as 5-15 minutes daily, rather than lengthy sessions sporadically. Integrating mindfulness into daily routines creates consistency.

Morning: Begin the day with mindful breathing, body scans, or stretching as you wake up. Use prompts like:

> "Notice how your body feels this morning."

Bedtime: Unwind before bed with yoga, gratitude journaling, or calming breathing. End the day reflecting:

> "What did you do today that made you feel proud?"

Transitions: When switching activities, pause to tune into the senses before moving on to the next task.

> "What do you hear/see/smell/feel right now?"

Chores: Add mindfulness into household tasks by encouraging full focus on each step rather than rushing.

> "Pay close attention when folding the towels."

Commutes: Listen to guided meditations or play observation games during car rides:

> "I spy something yellow!"

Homework: Incorporate mindful breathing between assignments or subjects to refocus attention. Use fidget toys to aid concentration.

Meals: Chew each bite thoroughly. Discuss flavors and textures. Notice emotions and sensations that arise.

Weaving brief practices throughout the day trains the mind to consistently return to the present moment.

CULTIVATING RESILIENCE THROUGH MINDFULNESS

The good news is mindfulness naturally builds many pillars of resilience in children, from concentration and adaptability to optimism and self-esteem. Some examples:

Focus:

> Mindfulness enhances executive functioning related to attention, working memory, and impulse control (Ninivaggi, 2019).

The ability to focus despite distractions creates perseverance.

Cognitive Flexibility:

Mindfulness teaches children to observe thoughts and emotions without attachment. This aids cognitive flexibility - adapting perspectives to suit changing situations (Council et al., 2015).

Calm:

By lowering stress hormone levels and activating the parasympathetic nervous system, mindfulness facilitates relaxation and emotional regulation (Tang, 2017b).

COMPOSURE PROMOTES RATIONAL DECISION-MAKING UNDER PRESSURE.

Optimism:

Mindfulness has been linked to greater positivity by reducing activity in the brain's default mode network associated with negative thinking (Greene et al., 2016).

An upbeat attitude facilitates resilience.

Self-Esteem:

Mindfully observing oneself without judgment cultivates self-acceptance and compassion. Kids become less reactive to perceived failures or criticism (Leary & Hoyle, 2013).

Healthy self-regard empowers inner strength.

Connection:

Mindfulness strengthens empathy and perspective-taking (Niemiec, 2023)

Feeling understood by others is a source of resilience during hardships.

Thus mindfulness provides children with skills to handle adversities and rapid changes with emotional balance and optimism.

SELF-REGULATION STRATEGIES

Parents can foster self-regulation through mindfulness techniques like:

Breath awareness: Have your child take 3-5 deep breaths when frustrated before reacting. The pause allows the prefrontal cortex to override the emotional limbic system.

. . .

"I Spy" games: Play **"I Spy"** during mundane tasks, having your child identify sights, sounds, and tastes.

> This engages bottom-up and top-down attention networks in the brain, enhancing self-control (Keengwe, 2022).

Body scans: Guide children to slowly scan their body from toes to head, relaxing each muscle group. This builds body awareness and calmness.

Walking meditation: Focus attention fully on the sensations of each step - heel, sole, toe. This directs the mind away from distractions and mind-wandering.

Expanding awareness: Teach children to deliberately expand their attention to take in their environment using all five senses. This awareness shrinks emotional reactivity.

Noting thoughts:

> Prompt children to silently label thoughts as "future," "past," or "imagined" when the mind wanders. This improves metacognition and refocuses attention (Fisk, 2018).

Through repetition, these techniques become automated, allowing children to self-regulate emotions, impulses, and behaviors.

BRAIN TRAINING FOR RESILIENCE

Emerging neuroscience reveals how mindfulness rewires the brain's neural pathways to build resilience from an early age. Some of the key effects include:

Enhanced prefrontal cortex functioning: As the brain's executive control center, the PFC governs planning, problem-solving, emotional regulation, and impulse control.

> Studies demonstrate experienced meditators have increased PFC activation (Bullock, 2016).
> These functions all support resilience.

Reduced amygdala activity: The amygdala is responsible for our stress responses and emotional reactivity.

> Mindfulness shrinks amygdala gray matter volume, reducing anxiety, fear and anger outbursts (Arden, 2010).

Kids become less overwhelmed by emotions.

· · ·

Increased insula activity: This region promotes body awareness and tuning into feelings.

> Greater insula density after mindfulness training helps children recognize and express their emotions skillfully (Eisendrath, 2016).

This emotional clarity bolsters self-regulation.

Reduced DMN activity:

> The default mode network (DMN) is responsible for mind-wandering and negative self-talk. Mindfulness correlated with less DMN activity, replacing unhelpful thinking with non-judgmental awareness (Langland-Hassan & Vicente, 2018).

Thus mindfulness reshapes the brain's structure and functioning to enhance composure, attention, emotional intelligence, and positivity - key components of resilience.

MINDFULNESS PRACTICES FOR DIFFERENT AGES

The following mindfulness practices are tailored for different age groups to match their attention spans and abilities:

Ages 2-5:
  - Short 1-3 minute guided meditations using imagery like bubbles rising and popping.

- Mindful movement exercises like animal poses, marching, or finger dances.

- Interactive breathing activities using pinwheels, bubble wands, or stuffed animal movements on the belly.

- Nature sensory exploration, like listening to leaves rustling or noticing cloud shapes.

Ages 6-9:
  - 5-7 minute breathing-focused meditations. Direct attention to the abdomen rising and falling.

- Muscle relaxation by tensing and releasing muscle groups one by one.

- Visualization adventures using stories engaging various senses.

- Focus on senses during daily routines - sounds during washing hands, textures while eating.

Ages 10-12:
- Guided imagery meditations for up to 10 minutes. Imagine soothing scenes like stargazing.

- Mindful art activities like mandala drawings.

- Gratitude or wisdom journaling before bedtime.

- Loving-kindness practices wishing self and others well-being.

Teens:
- 15-20 minute breath awareness sits.

- Walking meditation noticing movement sensations.

- Self-inquiry exercises like "What emotions arise today?" to build emotional awareness.

- Discuss mindfulness insights like impermanence.

- Yoga sequences to reduce anxiety and stress.

. . .

The key is making mindfulness accessible for their age by keeping it succinct, hands-on, and relatable. What matters most is consistency. Just 5 minutes daily confers cognitive and emotional benefits versus lengthy, irregular sessions.

CREATING A MINDFUL FAMILY ENVIRONMENT

For children to learn mindfulness as a life skill, they need to be in an environment where mindfulness is modeled, valued and enjoyed:

Practice together: Set aside 10 minutes each day for family mindfulness time. Take turns choosing fun, creative activities. Making it consistent family bonding time enhances motivation.

Be fully present: When interacting with your child, make a conscious effort to be attentively present without distractions like phones, laptops, or TVs. This model's mindful engagement.

Point out mindful moments: Verbally note small mindful moments throughout the day - pausing to listen to birds, the taste at the first bite of an apple, and a deep breath before starting homework. This builds awareness.

Share openly: Discuss your personal mindfulness experiences with kids. How did taking a calming break help you at work today? Let them see mindfulness in action.

. . .

Reinforce mindfully: Praise mindful behaviors like pausing before reacting or showing compassion. Don't force formal practice, but positively reinforce mindful habits.

Explain gently: If your child resists practicing, gently convey why mindfulness matters to you but don't pressure. Just model mindfulness in daily life.

Be flexible: Offer shorter practices some days or incorporate mindful habits like eating slowly. Rigidity sabotages motivation. Keep it accommodating.

Stay patient: Children may be inconsistent as their skills develop. Trust this winding process. Your steady guidance and compassion nurture their progress.

By infusing mindfulness consistently into your family culture, children's brains wire mindfulness into their neural circuitry, gradually transforming reactive patterns into mindful responses.

MINDFULNESS GAMES FOR BUILDING RESILIENCE

Fun, interactive mindfulness games engage kids in building resilience skills:

Jenga with "mindful" blocks: This classic game trains concentration, calm during challenges, and recovery from setbacks.

Paint some blocks with words like **"breathe"** or **"stay calm"** to pull out for mindful reminders.

Loving-kindness bingo: Create bingo cards with positive wishes like **"feel safe," "find joy,"** and **"laugh often."** Take turns calling out wishes and filling cards to build compassion for yourself and others.

Mindful movement freeze dance: Play music and dance freely, then pause the music and have kids freeze and tune into their senses before resuming. Practices stopping reactively and cultivates awareness.

Gratitude charades: Have children silently act out things or people they are grateful for and guess each other's responses. Boosts positivity and perspective-taking.

Overcoming obstacles: Use toys like Lego people or dolls to depict calming down and problem-solving challenges. Constructive play strengthens coping skills.

Soap bubble deep breathing: Blowing bubbles to a slow count keeps children focused on the breath. Popping bubbles represent letting go of worries.

. . .

Preparing kids for life's curveballs with mindfulness builds their inner resources. Then when challenges arise, they have the skills to respond adaptively and bounce back wiser and stronger!

TROUBLESHOOTING COMMON OBSTACLES

When teaching children mindfulness, you may encounter these typical challenges:

The child seems bored or restless: Keep it playful! Add sensory props, imaginary journeys, and challenges to maintain curiosity. Celebrate small successes.

Too much energy to sit still: Incorporate stretching, simple yoga, or walking meditation. Practice after physical play when energy levels are lower.

Short attention span: Start with 1-2 minutes and work up gradually. Use repetition, captivating imagery, music, and positive reinforcement to sustain attention.

Self-consciousness: Explain distraction is natural. Share your own learning process. Keep it low-pressure. Practice alongside them.

. . .

Impatience with slow progress: Every child has a unique path. Effort and small steps forward confer benefits. Remain compassionately patient and flexible.

Judging themselves or comparing: Teach non-judgment as a core part of mindfulness. Emphasize that each experience is unique. Celebrate their own progress.

With empathy and creativity, you can navigate any bumps that arise, helping children cultivate mindfulness as a lifelong inner compass.

CONCLUSION

In summary, mindfulness is invaluable for developing executive functioning, resilience, focus, optimism, emotional regulation, and compassion. By practicing mindfulness tailored to children's developmental needs, parents strengthen the neural wiring that bolsters resilience and self-regulation from an early age. Making mindfulness playful, consistent, and engaging helps children embrace it. Over time, these daily habits become lifelong skills children can draw upon to skillfully navigate adversity and thrive. Mindfulness provides an inner toolkit enabling them to handle life's curveballs with flexibility, equilibrium, and hope.

PART 2: INTRODUCING MEDITATION TO CHILDREN THROUGH STORIES

STORIES FOR CHILDREN TO HELP THEM UNDERSTAND MEDITATION TECHNIQUES

INTRODUCING CHILDREN TO MEDITATION THROUGH ENCHANTING STORIES
- "The Butterfly Garden: Where Magic Takes Flight"
- "The Magic Forest: A Journey of Imagination"
- "The Ocean Waves: A Relaxing Adventure"

Meditation Through More Enchanting Stories
- "The Wise Tree"
- "The Odyssey of the Mindful Voyager"
- "The Magic Breath"
- "The Rainbow of Emotions"
- "The Gratitude Garden"
- "The Ants"
- "The Family Garden"
- "The Mindful Explorer"

CHAPTER 6
STORIES FOR CHILDREN TO HELP THEM UNDERSTAND MEDITATION TECHNIQUES
USING STORIES TO INTRODUCE MEDITATION TO CHILDREN

STORIES HAVE a timeless power to spark imagination, convey wisdom, and connect us profoundly to the human experience. It is no surprise, then, that storytelling provides a natural conduit for imparting the benefits of meditation to children in an engaging, relatable manner.

In this chapter, we explore how narratives with embedded mindfulness techniques can serve as a catalyst for children to embrace meditation. Parents can plant seeds of lifelong well-being and self-care by infusing stories with lessons on focus, emotional awareness, visualization, and relaxation. We aim to provide a toolkit of sample stories, exercises, and strategies for leveraging the magic of storytelling to nurture mindfulness in children.

THE POWER OF STORIES

For millennia across cultures, the oral tradition of storytelling served both to entertain and educate.

> According to parenting expert, "Stories build sustained focus, activate the imagination, develop listening skills, and teach children to recognize emotions and new perspectives." (Yogman et al., 2018)
>
> Neuroscience demonstrates that narrative transportation enhances neural activity related to visualization, empathy, and immersion. (Bohr & Memarzadeh, 2020)

Stories enable kids to absorb new information and values seamlessly by embedding lessons within compelling characters and plots. Children invest deeply in tales that whisk them to enchanted worlds and intriguing adventures.

> As education specialists note, "The story structure provides a framework that helps children to contextualize, personalize, and internalize new concepts" (Douglass, 2018)

The inherent enjoyment of listening to a captivating tale taps into kids' playful disposition. When meditation techniques are thoughtfully woven into stories, children incorporate mindfulness through imagination rather than didactic techniques alone. Repetition across various narratives ingrains these tools into their worldview in an integrated, lasting manner.

INTRODUCING MINDFULNESS MEDITATION

Mindfulness meditation teaches present-moment awareness with openness and curiosity.

According to psychologist Dr. Whitney Stewart, "Practicing mindfulness improves children's ability to pay attention, manage emotions, reduce stress, and cultivate compassion" (Stewart, 2021).

Kids naturally inhabit the here and now, making mindfulness an intuitive practice.

Short stories like **"A Walk in the Woods"** can model mindfulness in action:

It was a sunny Saturday morning, and Mia and her mom headed out to the nature trail near their house. As they began their walk at a leisurely pace, Mia focused on how the air felt against her skin and listened to the leaves softly crunching beneath her feet.

"Take my hand, Mia."

Her mom said gently. Mia slid her hand into her mom's palm and noticed how warm and comforting it felt.

Up ahead, a bluebird's melody flowed through the trees. Mia tuned into the sweet trilling notes as she felt a cool breeze graze her cheeks. She watched the swaying wildflowers without judging them as pretty or plain, simply noticing their dance.

"Let's take a moment here to breathe deeply."

Her mom suggested, inhaling the fresh forest air. As Mia breathed slowly in and out, she sensed a spreading calmness within.

Continuing along the trail, Mia observed nature with curiosity and delight, feeling fully part of its tapestry. This magical forest walk showed Mia that by tuning into her senses and surroundings without judgment, the whole world could fill her with wonder.

THIS STORY MODELED:

- Tuning into the five senses
    - Focusing on the present
    - Non-judgmental awareness
    - Using the breath to anchor attention

To reinforce the concepts, parents can guide children through a brief mindfulness exercise afterward:

- Find a comfortable seated position and close your eyes
    - Bring attention to your breath as it enters and leaves your body
    - Notice any sensations, sights, or sounds in this moment
    - If your mind wanders, gently return your focus to your breath
    - When ready, open your eyes and reflect on what you noticed

Using imagination to convey mindfulness allows children to integrate the principles actively through visualization. Repetition with various characters and scenarios anchors it as a life skill.

RELAXATION THROUGH STORYTELLING

While many equate meditation with calmness, specific relaxation techniques can also be taught through stories. Progressive muscle relaxation involves tensing and relaxing muscle groups systematically to release tension. Breathing exercises that use imagery of colors, nature scenes, or gentle movement of the breath can also induce relaxation.

The story below guides children through relaxation using the metaphor of floating on clouds:

Layla gazes out the window at the soft white clouds drifting across the blue sky. She decides to imagine floating away on a cloud and see how relaxed she can feel.

Layla lies down on her back and breathes deeply as a cloud glides down and gently scoops her up. It carries her into the sky, slowing all of her thoughts and worries.

As the cloud floats along, Layla feels herself becoming lighter and more peaceful. She lets her toes uncurl, and her legs feel soft and relaxed. Her arms get heavier and heavier, sinking into the plush cloud.

The clouds around her take on shapes of hearts, stars, and circles as she drifts through the sky. Looking at these shapes, Layla's eyes feel more and more relaxed.

. . .

Her floating cloud rocks her gently from side to side, and her neck feels looser and looser. Her back feels supported, and her shoulders melt into the softness.

With each breath, Layla feels more calm and rested. Her cloud friend is carrying her to a world of total relaxation as she breathes deeply.

This tranquil journey showed Layla how calming breathing and imagining her body at rest could make her feel peaceful and centered. She learned she could find this relaxation anytime she needed it.

THIS STORY USES IMAGERY TO DEMONSTRATE:
- Deep breathing
    - Progressive muscle relaxation
    - Peaceful visualization

To deepen learning, parents can lead children in a relaxation exercise afterward:

- Lie down in a comfortable position
    - Take slow, full breaths letting the body relax
    - Clench and release different muscles one at a time
    - Imagine floating on a soft cloud or in a gentle boat as you breathe

- When ready, return your awareness to the room

Through relatable characters and scenarios, stories provide an immersive platform for kids to experience firsthand how relaxation techniques can calm the mind and body. Repetition builds their skills.

VISUALIZATION FOR INNER EXPLORATION

Visualization, or guided imagery, leverages the imagination to conjure vivid sensory experiences.

> Studies show visualization enhances neural activity in the brain's sensory areas, allowing children to engage inner realms (Arden, 2010b) deeply.

Tales can become springboards for children to cultivate peaceful inner worlds actively.

The story below illustrates how a child uses her imagination to create an inner sanctuary:

One night, as Layla snuggled into her cozy bed, she decided to picture her favorite imaginary sanctuary to help her drift peacefully off to sleep.

. . .

Layla closed her eyes and imagined walking along a forest path blanketed in vibrant green moss. Up ahead, she discovered her own little cottage nestled among pine trees. As she opened the rounded wooden door, she smelled the comforting scent of ginger tea brewing on the stove.

Looking around the single-room cottage, Layla saw her favorite books on the shelves, comfy pillows on the window bench, and a small desk for writing. She knew this was a place all her own where she could feel safe, cozy, and creative.

Layla climbed into the cottage bed as sunlight streamed through the window, bathing her in warmth. Curled beneath the patchwork quilt, Layla felt herself relaxing completely. She had found her own magical sanctuary within.

This inner world was a gift Layla could call upon at any time to find serenity, joy, or inspiration. Now she looked forward to the adventures her imagination would bring!

THIS STORY DEMONSTRATES HOW VISUALIZATION CAN:

- Promote relaxation
    - Spark creativity
    - Offer a mental refuge
    - Build imagination

To encourage children's exploration, guide them in creating their own inner sanctuaries:

. . .

- Find a comfortable position, close your eyes, and take a few slow breaths
    - Imagine a place that feels special just for you - maybe a secret garden or seaside cottage
    - Picture the details - the sights, textures, and smells that make it feel welcoming
    - Know this space will be waiting within whenever you need comfort or inspiration

Leveraging imagination helps children realize they can access serene inner worlds anytime. Visualization exercises strengthen creativity and self-awareness.

THE JOURNEY AHEAD

Stories can smooth children's introduction to meditation in countless ways, weaving it into the fabric of their lives. Tales reduce any perceived mystique around concepts like mindfulness, relaxation, or inner reflection. Over time, children come to intuitively practice techniques as part of their daily repertoire rather than a forced routine.

Stories speak the language of a child's heart. Their inherent appeal makes them ideal vehicles for imparting self-care skills in a gradual, integrated manner. By meeting children where they are developmentally with engaging narratives and follow-up exercises, we plant seeds that blossom into lifelong habits as naturally as their bedtime story rituals.

. . .

This book has aimed to provide you with resources to begin tapping into the power of storytelling as a catalyst for nurturing mindfulness. We hope the stories, exercises, and techniques spark your own creativity. Every child has a unique inner world. Tailor tales that resonate with your child's interests and tendencies.

Like a sage storyteller passing down wisdom, you have the privilege of gifting your child with the inner tools to thrive. May the chapters ahead enchant and inspire you to further unlock storytelling's potential for imparting the gifts of mindfulness? When we speak to children's hearts, their journey unfolds with delight.

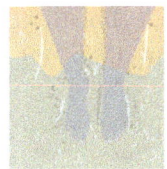

CHAPTER 7
INTRODUCING CHILDREN TO MEDITATION THROUGH ENCHANTING STORIES

STORIES HAVE a wonderful way of sparking imagination and conveying meaningful lessons in an engaging manner. As parents and caregivers, we can harness the power of storytelling to introduce children to meditation in a relatable way.

In this chapter, we will explore three sample stories that creatively integrate mindfulness, visualization, and relaxation techniques. By infusing these concepts into imaginative tales, children can absorb key meditation principles while embarking on delightful adventures.

THE STORIES WE WILL HIGHLIGHT INCLUDE:

The Butterfly Garden: A Magical Adventure in Mindfulness

This story whisks children away to an enchanted garden filled with butterflies. As they immerse themselves in this vibrant setting, children learn about focusing their senses on the present moment, observing nature without judgment, and using their breath to anchor attention. This story offers an accessible introduction to mindfulness meditation.

The Magic Forest: A Journey of Imagination and Calm

In this tale, children visualize walking through a peaceful forest, noticing its sights, sounds, and textures. As they breathe deeply, they experience a sense of serenity and calm. This story demonstrates the power of visualization to transport children to tranquil inner realms where they can release stress.

The Ocean Waves: A Serene Journey to Relaxation

Children imagine lying on the beach listening to soothing ocean waves. As they envision the waves carrying tension away on each exhale, they learn how to systematically relax their body and mind. This story provides an immersive way for kids to explore relaxation techniques.

These three sample stories illustrate how parents can spark children's interest in meditation by weaving key concepts into imaginative adventures. The playful narratives help demystify practices like mindfulness, visualization, and relaxation through characters children relate to. After sharing these tales, engaging children in integrated exercises further, cements the skills being conveyed.

Let us now dive into each enchanting story, discovering how storytelling can ignite children's curiosity and lay the foundation for a lifelong practice of nurturing inner peace and emotional well-being through meditation. By meeting children where they are, these stories transform meditation into a world of possibility rather than abstraction.

"THE BUTTERFLY GARDEN: WHERE MAGIC TAKES FLIGHT"
STORYTIME:

© 2023 Foss Plus. All rights reserved.

The Butterfly Garden: A Magical Adventure in Mindfulness

Once upon a time, nestled deep within an ancient forest, there existed a secret sanctuary known as the Butterfly Garden. This mystical oasis was home to hundreds of kaleidoscopic butterflies that fluttered and danced among the trees and flowers.

The garden radiated a celestial aura that drew curious explorers to its wonder. Among them were two young friends named Lily and Martin, whose sense of adventure led them to its hidden entrance each sunny morning.

On one particularly glorious day, as Lily and Martin wandered through the muted forest light, a vibrant monarch butterfly with wings like stained glass alighted gently on Lily's outstretched finger.

> "Martin, look!"

She exclaimed in hushed delight.

> "Have you ever seen anything so beautiful?"

Martin leaned in to admire the butterfly's intricate orange and black patterns, the delicate symmetry of its wings.

> "It's amazing."

He whispered back.

> "I wonder what it feels like to be so light and free."

As the monarch took flight once more, the friends exchanged a glance brimming with possibility. Today their footsteps would find the enchanted Butterfly Garden.

Guided by curiosity and wonder, Lily and Martin ventured deeper into the woodland realm. Dappled sunlight illuminated their path as the trees opened up to reveal the garden in all its splendor.

Lily's sharp intake of breath was the only sound breaking the mystical silence. Before they unfolded a meadow dotted with wildflowers, each petal alight in vivid color. Hundreds of butterflies glided on the sweet breeze, their wings kaleidoscopes of living rainbows.

"It's magic,"

Lily finally breathed, turning slowly to absorb every detail. She felt she had stepped into a dreamscape too stunning to be real.

Beside her, Martin shut his eyes and inhaled deeply, sensing the energy that hummed through this space.

"Can you feel it, Lily?"

He asked with a smile.

"The enchantment in the air?"

Lily clasped her hands as if in prayer.

"It's like a thread of wonder is woven into everything here."

She replied in awe.

"Even the silence seems to shimmer with mindfulness."

Unable to resist exploring, the two stepped gingerly into the meadow, careful not to disturb its tranquility. Butterflies sang past in silence, carried on shimmering wings.

"What do you see?"

Martin asked, knowing Lily's artist's eye would uncover beauty he might overlook.

Lily peered closely, noticing vivid new details.

> "Emerald swallowtails are sipping nectar, and orange monarchs are sunning on rocks. Oh! And that one - a morpho with wings like living sapphires!"

Each new discovery left her more enraptured. Martin nodded approvingly.

> "Now tune your other senses too. What do you feel in this place?"

Kneeling slowly, Lily caressed the soft meadow grasses, then cradled a delicate aster bloom in her palm. Its symmetry and velvet texture fascinated her. On impulse, she suddenly leaped up, twirling with outstretched arms as laughter spilled from her lips.

Martin grinned, catching some of her glee.

> "I think someone is feeling pure joy!"

Lily paused to catch her breath, still tingling with elation.

> "You're right, I feel so happy and free here!"

The simple act of unfettered play had awakened something joyful within.

> "Now, listen closely,"

Martin instructed next. As Lily quieted herself, the garden

seemed to amplify its melodies - humming bees, rustling leaves, and the hypnotic flutter of wings all composed a symphony of tranquility.

"It's the most beautiful music,"

Lily remarked, loathe to break the spell. Even the silence itself sang with life.

"And finally, breathe deeply,"

said, Martin. As Lily inhaled, the meadow's heady floral perfume filled her senses, its sweetness underscored by rich earth. With each breath, she felt the tension leave her body.

Opening her eyes, Lily saw Martin regarding her warmly.

"You understand now, don't you?"

he asked.

"This garden lives fully in each moment, awakening our senses if we let it. When we're present, we're as free as the butterflies."

Lily nodded slowly, the lessons of the garden imprinting themselves on her spirit. Each vivid sensation celebrated the joy of living in the now.

"Can we stay awhile?"

She implored Martin, who nodded amicably. Finding a birch tree, they settled together to watch the butterflies' hypnotic choreography.

Lily soon lost track of time observing their shimmering ballet. But as the sun dipped low on the horizon, she knew their time in this magical place was ending.

> "Thank you for sharing this with me."

Lily said softly to Martin as they rose reluctantly.

> "I'll treasure this gift of mindfulness in my heart always."

As the last rays of sun lit the meadow, a monarch glided past them in farewell. Lily whispered,

> "Until we meet again."

As the ancient forest folded them safely in its embrace once more.

But now, a seed of the Butterfly Garden's enchantment nestled in Lily's soul. In days to come, whenever she needed to center herself, she would shut her eyes and find herself transported back to that sunlit meadow.

Martin, too, would drift back on memory's wings whenever chaos encroached too close. Together they had absorbed a vital truth - by opening their senses and embracing the present, they could unlock the beauty and magic inherent in each moment.

Thus the two friends carried the Butterfly Garden's gifts with them wherever they wandered. Its lessons continued shaping them even long after childhood slipped away.

When Lily found her mood turning dark as storm clouds, she'd stop to touch a flower or savor a mouthful of peach, calling back that joy. When Martin lost perspective, the metallic glint of a butterfly's wing could restore it.

And in fleeting, unguarded moments, they would catch each other's eye, remembering two children who once entered an enchanted garden and discovered wonder lived not in distant realms but within their very senses.

So the Butterfly Garden lived on, blooming in their hearts wherever they went. For its magic had shown them that to fully participate in life, one had only to awaken their eyes and discover the singular miracle that is this moment. All else unfolds from there.

The end.

Remember, my dear young readers, the power of mindfulness lies within you. Just like Lily and Martin, you can embark on magical adventures in your imagination, exploring the wonders of the world and finding peace in the present moment.

"THE MAGIC FOREST: A JOURNEY OF IMAGINATION"
STORYTIME:

© 2023 Manon Doucet. All rights reserved.

Lucy's Forest Adventure

It was a bright summer morning when young Lucy skipped out her front door, ready for adventure. Breathing deeply of the fresh air, she set off straight for the forest at the edge of town.

Lucy loved exploring the wooded trails and stumbling upon hidden surprises deep in the trees. The shady forest paths offered such a contrast to the noisy, crowded streets of her neighborhood.

As Lucy entered the forest's embrace, she was enveloped by stillness and serenity. High overhead, birds trilled sweet melodies. A gentle breeze set the leaves aflutter, their whispers the only sound.

Breathing deeply of the pine-scented air, Lucy felt a sense of calm wash over her. The forest's tranquility was just what her busy mind needed.

The winding trail brought Lucy to a sun-dappled clearing, its long grasses, and wildflowers swaying in the breeze. Shielding her eyes, she turned her face up to admire the cloudless blue sky.

Overcome with delight, Lucy closed her eyes and spread her arms wide, embracing the meadow. The sun's warmth danced across her skin. Giggling, she began to twirl with arms outstretched, hair fanning out around her. Round and round, she spun until dizzily collapsing onto the soft grass.

Laying there, Lucy thought if she could freeze this moment of pure joy and lightness, she would. The meadow's beauty energized her body and soul.

When she could twirl no more, Lucy continued on her way. The forest deepened around her, and the trees clustered closer. Sunbeams streamed through the canopy like enchanted spotlights meant just for her.

Lucy imagined herself journeying into a magical realm. She followed a chattering stream spanned by fallen logs. Mossy stones disturbed the water's glassy surface as it babbled over them.

Coming upon a still, mirror-like pool, Lucy knelt at its edge, captivated. Silver minnows darted beneath the surface, catching glints of sunlight. She trailed her fingers through the cool water, sending gentle ripples across its face.

After lingering seaside, Lucy continued down the wooded trail. Here the ancient trees towered like giants from a fairy tale. Their gnarled branches wove together, creating a shaded canopy overhead.

Lucy craned her neck, taking in their enormity. Placing a palm against one enormous trunk, she felt the strength and history rooted in its wood. What tales these elders could tell!

Kneeling, Lucy explored the forest floor, observing networks of tree roots and delicate ferns uncurling their lacy fronds. She imagined herself tiny enough to get lost in their miniature forests. A whole world of discovery lay there.

The trail led Lucy deeper still into rays of golden light filtering down from the thick canopy. Her footsteps landed without sound on the soft earth. In the hushed air, she could hear a bird trilling an enchanting melody somewhere up ahead.

Turning a corner, Lucy drew a sharp breath, frozen in place. A waterfall tumbled from on high, its crystalline waters scattering rainbows in the mist. Delicate orchids in vibrant shades of fuchsia, violet, and azure lined the banks. An invisible chorus of birdsong serenaded the idyllic scene.

Finding a hidden nook beneath trailing willow branches, Lucy sank down and shut her eyes. She allowed the sounds of the waterfall and birdsong to fill her senses. Her busy thoughts slowed to match the tranquil tempo of this natural sanctuary.

After an indeterminate time, Lucy rose and balanced on the rocky bank, taking in the waterfall's full majesty. Below, the churning waters emptied into a crystal clear pool. Looking down, Lucy saw clouds drifting across a mirrored sky.

Turning, she observed the ancient forest stretching unbroken to the horizon. Lucy closed her eyes once more and envisioned roots extending from her body into the rich earth, connecting her to the land. She held this moment in her heart like a treasure.

The day was waning, so Lucy reluctantly turned homeward. With every step, she absorbed the tranquility of the living forest. Its energy lingered within her like a song stuck fast in her mind.

Back home, Lucy's creative spirit awoke. She grabbed her art supplies and began recreating her magical journey on paper - the sun-drenched meadow, winding stream, majestic trees, and hidden waterfall. With each drawing, she imprinted the magic on her heart.

That night, Lucy dreamed of soaring over the forest like a bird, carried on wings of her imagination. The wisp of a melody followed her into slumber - the forest's gift bestowed on a child who knew how to listen.

The next sunny morning found Lucy racing back to the forest, eager to continue her exploration. She chased the dappled light along twisting trails, discovered feathered friends in the willows, and breathed deep the scent of moss and earth.

The woods became her refuge, where she found both adventure and tranquility. After the noisiest, most chaotic days, Lucy would return here. As the trees soothed her frustrations, she would once again find her center.

When Lucy had a daughter of her own, she shared this gift, leading the child down shady trails and teaching her to listen. She watched her daughter stand beneath towering trees, eyes full of wonder, and knew the forest had roots in her heart now too.

Decades later, when Lucy's hair was silver and her steps slower, she would retreat to her woods. There she would sit with eyes closed, feeling time fall away until she was just a girl again, enthralled by nature's magic.

The wise old trees she had known since childhood remained, their constancy and strength anchoring her like always. They, too, had grown, though at a more patient pace. Lucy laid her hand on ridges layered through their bark, each circle representing a full turn of seasons.

"Thank you"

She whispered, expressing gratitude and transcending words. The leaves fluttered overhead, sunlight winking through.

When Lucy was gone, her gift lived on. Her great-granddaughter ran through springy moss and held tight to her grandmother's hand. And so it continued.

Lucy's forest remained, its tranquility beckoning children of every new era. They learned what she had known - that wonder resides not in far-off places but rather within an open heart. All that's required is the willingness to listen.

The End

"THE OCEAN WAVES: A RELAXING ADVENTURE"
STORYTIME:

© 2023 Manon Doucet. All rights reserved.

The Ocean Waves: A Serene Journey to Relaxation

Our story begins on a tranquil evening with two best friends, Mia and Noah. The adventurous young pair lay side by side on rainbow-striped beach towels, eyes fixed on the first twinkling stars emerging in the dusky sky.

As the tide gently lapped the shore, Noah said introspectively,

> "Do you ever feel like the ocean waves have a calming effect on you, Mia?"

Mia smiled softly, the moonlight dancing in her eyes.

> "Absolutely,"

she replied.

> "The sea has a way of soothing my soul and washing worries far from shore."

Noah nodded thoughtfully. Then his face lit up.

> "I have an idea! Why don't we close our eyes and imagine sailing away to a peaceful paradise?"

Mia's grin widened.

> "A visualization journey? I'm in!"

She settled onto her back, hands laced on her stomach, as Noah mirrored her posture.

Mia began narrating in a hushed, peaceful voice.

> "Picture yourself lying on the softest, warmest sand you've ever felt. Gentle waves lap soothingly at your toes, serenading you."

Noah inhaled deeply, imagining the sweet salt-air scent. As he slowly exhaled, his stresses drifted away on the breeze. In his mind's eye, he saw tangerine and pink streaks painting the evening sky. He heard the peaceful swoosh of waves and cries of wheeling gulls.

> "How does the beach look and feel?"

asked Mia.

> "It's flawless,"

Noah sighed blissfully.

> "The water glitters like jewels. The sand embraces me like a downy blanket."

Mia joined Noah in the tranquil vision. Together they strolled barefoot along the shore as the fading light transformed the tide pools into liquid rainbows. They built mighty castles adorned with seashells and launched kites that danced on the salty wind.

With each passing moment, their bodies felt lighter, their minds clearer. A profound sense of peace radiated through them, as soothing as the tide's steady rhythm.

When glittering stars adorned the sky like jewels, they opened their eyes reluctantly, the vision fading. Yet its tranquility lingered within.

Noah gave Mia's hand a grateful squeeze.

> "That was rejuvenating! My mind feels refreshed and calm."

> "Mine too,"

Mia replied, stifling a yawn.

> "The sea has healing magic."

As they gathered their towels, the real waves sang their timeless lullaby. The friends departed energized, spirits glowing like the moon's soft light.

The next week was chaotic for Mia and Noah. So much homework! Social drama! Chores and tasks! They barely had time to think.

By Friday, both felt absolutely spent. As they trudged home from school, Mia turned to Noah.

> "Remember our beach visualization? Can we go there again?"

Noah nearly wilted with relief.

> "Yes! I've been needing some relaxation therapy."

They hurried to their tranquil spot, snuggling into the cool sand. Mia's voice drifted softly through the air, conjuring details of breeze and waves and gulls. Noah inhaled the imagined scent of honeysuckle, feeling the tension drain from his body.

They built ornate castles swirled with seashells and braided seaweed tapestries. They floated effortlessly in the shimmering tide pools. Each moment washed them in deeper peace.

Too soon, the stars signaled it was time to return. Noah and Mia's eyes fluttered open slowly, wheels still turning in the sea-soaked scene.

> "That magic is desperately needed this week,"

Noah said.

Mia nodded, gathering her towel.

> "This visualization is the perfect escape for restoring balance to stressful times."

The ocean continued its soothing lullaby as they headed home with lighter steps.

Whenever chaos loomed, they returned to their secret seaside sanctuary within. Soon, they realized its power could also calm troubled hearts around them.

One day, Mia found her sister Lea in tears over a bad test grade that threatened her scholarship. Taking Lea's hands, Mia slowly guided her through the beach vision - the salty air, the cotton-candy sunset, the lull of gliding waves. Soon Lea's tears ceased, and her breath steadied.

> "That was beautiful,"

she murmured.

> "I feel like I just had a massage!"

Noah, too, began sharing the breathing and visualization exercises with his anxious cousin Ben. Focusing on the detailed serene scenes gave Ben's worried mind a rest.

> "Thanks, Noah,"

Ben said.

> "I really needed that calm place today."

And so the friends realized their tranquil seaside retreat could soothe any soul in need - a sheltering port in a storm.

Years passed, and Mia became a clinical therapist. But she noticed modern approaches left some patients' deeper spiritual needs untouched.

So she again called upon the wisdom of the waves, leading clients through meditations to that secret shore. The positive results were soon undeniable.

One grateful patient told Mia,

> "I was drowning in stress and worry before our sessions. Now it feels like coming up for air."

Noah became a teacher and found his students, too, benefited from the mindfulness of the present moment that the beach vision cultivated. The sea sounds and sensations effectively quieted busy minds.

And within themselves, the friends still returned often to that inner shore. They knew its healing magic was always accessible from within. It needed only to be remembered.

When Mia retired, she moved to a cottage by the ocean. Sitting on the weathered deck each morning, a mug of tea in hand, she smiled, remembering two children who once dreamed under the stars.

The crashing waves sang their timeless song. But in a way, the real beach now seemed an echo of the one she and Noah had visited so often in their minds.

Mia understood the true power had been their imagination, transforming the sea's beauty into a landscape of healing. They had tapped into an inner wisdom as eternal as the tides.

Now she watched the sunrise paint the sky in pastels, her heart filled with gratitude. However, life flowed like the waves; this she knew - inner peace was only a deep breath away.

The end.

A SPECIAL NOTE FROM MANON DOUCET

Hello, dear reader!

First and foremost, **thank you**. By diving into the pages of my book, you've allowed my words, my heart, and my imagination to become a part of your world. For that, I'm endlessly grateful.

Did this tale whisk you away on an adventure, spark an emotion, or leave an impression? If so, I'd love to hear about it!

Here's how you can share your thoughts:

Revisit the platform where you found this book. Be it Amazon, Kobo, Barns and Nobles, Apple Books, Google Play or any other cozy corner of the literary world.

Remember, your insights might be the guiding star for another reader in search of their next read!

Click 'Submit'. Just like that, you've made a difference. Your voice might inspire someone else to embark on the same journey you did.

Your reflections not only light the way for future readers but also warm the hearts of authors like me, encouraging us to keep dreaming, writing, and sharing. It's a beautiful ripple effect, and it starts with you.

From the bottom of my heart, thank you for sharing this literary voyage with me. Here's to many more tales, adventures, and moments shared through the magic of words!

With warmth and gratitude,

Manon Doucet

CHAPTER 8
MEDITATION THROUGH MORE ENCHANTING STORIES
THE STORIES WE WILL HIGHLIGHT INCLUDE:

"The Wise Tree"

THIS STORY PERSONIFIES a majestic tree as a source of wisdom, stillness, and stability. It serves as a gentle metaphor for how meditation allows us to connect to inner peace. The tale provides a simple yet profound understanding of meditation.

"The Odyssey of the Mindful Voyager"

In this action-packed story, children join their caregivers on an exciting mindfulness journey. As they navigate imagined landscapes, they learn to tap into a mindful state during various adventures. The tale empowers kids to view mindfulness as a companion through life.

"The Magic Breath"

Through endearing fantasy characters, this story demystifies conscious breathing techniques for anxious young minds. It provides children with a playful introduction to using their breath as an anchor during meditation.

"The Rainbow of Emotions"

This colorful tale explores the varied spectrum of children's emotions. It teaches how meditation helps cultivate awareness and acceptance of feelings. The story provides a creative framework for emotional intelligence and self-regulation.

"The Gratitude Garden"

In this vibrant story, a beautiful garden serves as the setting for practicing gratitude. Children imagine planting and tending to this garden, visualizing gratitude taking root in their hearts and blossoming into mindfulness.

"The Ants"

This lighthearted ant voyage guides children through an imaginative meditation centered on concentration. Playful narratives about leaves falling demonstrate how to gently return focus when the mind wanders. The tale makes meditation relatable.

"The Family Garden"

This heartwarming narrative invites the whole family to envision gardening together. It underscores practicing meditation as a shared activity and a special bonding ritual. The story sparks creativity for mindfully connecting as a family.

"The Mindful Explorer"

In this adventure, children wander their surroundings with curiosity and wonder. It emphasizes the spirit of mindfulness - being fully present and appreciative of each moment. The story reveals how mindfulness permeates our everyday lives.

Let us now dive into these rich stories, discovering how we can reveal the gift of mindfulness to children by speaking the language they know best - imagination. May these tales inspire you to further unlock storytelling's potential for imparting mindfulness in your family.

"THE WISE TREE"
STORYTIME:

© 2023 Foss Plus. All rights reserved.

"The Wise Tree: A Tale of Inner Calm"

Once upon a time, in a magical forest far, far away, there stood a tree unlike any other. This ancient tree was known as the Wise Tree, and it possessed great wisdom and tranquility. Its sturdy branches reached high into the azure sky, while its twisted roots delved deep into the fertile earth, grounding it firmly.

The Wise Tree had observed the passage of countless seasons and the comings and goings of many woodland creatures. Over time, it had learned to find serenity within itself, embracing stillness and attuning to the gentle whispers of the forest. The animals of the woodlands knew they could always find solace resting in the shade of the Wise Tree's canopy.

One sunny spring morning, a mother named Sarah decided to take her curious young daughter, Lily, on a special journey to meet the legendary Wise Tree. As they trekked through the lush forest, sunlight dappling the leafy trail, Sarah explained her intention behind this outing.

> "Lily, I want to share with you the tale of the Wise Tree. It has many lessons to teach about finding inner calm and strength even during life's tempests."

Sarah said.
Lily's amber eyes shone with curiosity.

> "Tell me more, Mommy! What makes the Wise Tree so special?"

she asked.

Sarah smiled gently at her daughter's eagerness.

> "Well, my dear, while the Wise Tree is ancient, its trunk gnarled and knotted with time, it radiates a sense of peace. This tree understands that true wisdom comes from within. When challenges arise, the Wise Tree remains deeply rooted and centered. It sways gracefully with the winds but does not break."

Enraptured, Lily tilted her head.

> "How does the tree stay so calm, Mommy?"

> "Through the practice of meditation,"

explained Sarah.

> "Meditation helps quiet our busy minds and tune into our inner selves. It allows us to find an oasis of tranquility amidst life's storms."

> "I want to learn how to do that!"

exclaimed Lily. Her face lit up with possibility.

> "Can you teach me to meditate like the Wise Tree, Mommy?"

Sarah smiled warmly, taking her daughter's small hand.

> "Of course, my dear. The Wise Tree has much wisdom to share if we are open to receiving it. Are you ready for a magical adventure?"

> "Yes, yes, yes!"

Shouted Lily gleefully. And with that, they continued their woodland journey.

Before long, Sarah and Lily arrived at a sun-dappled clearing where the Wise Tree stood tall. Lily's eyes grew wide with awe. The colossal trunk was ridged with age, and its thick branches reached skyward like gnarled hands grasping at clouds. A canopy of emerald green leaves rustled gently overhead.

Lily and Sarah found a soft patch of moss at the base of the towering tree. They sat together cross-legged, the cool forest breeze kissing their skin. Specks of sunlight danced through the leaves, dappling the ground.

Settling into stillness, Sarah said,

> "Let's begin our tree meditation, Lily. Close your eyes and take a deep, nourishing breath through your nose. Feel your belly expand like a balloon."

Lily inhaled slowly, picturing her tummy inflating.

> "Now gently release the breath through your mouth. Imagine you are a mighty tree, your leaves fluttering in the wind,"

instructed Sarah.

Lily exhaled calmly, envisioning the Wise Tree's leaves gliding downward on the breeze.

> "Breathe in tranquility; breathe out tension,"

guided Sarah.

Together, they continued this cycle, breathing in positive energy and exhaling any stress or worries from their minds and bodies. With each breath, Lily felt her muscles relaxing and her busy thoughts quieting.

> "Now, tune your senses to the sounds around you."

Said Sarah, her voice soft and peaceful.

> "Hear the birds sweetly singing and the wind dancing through the leaves."

Lily focused intently on the soothing melodies of the forest -

rustling leaves, chirping birds, and the creaking boughs of the Wise Tree. Each sound seemed to calm the chatter in her mind.

> "Feel the solid strength of the tree at your back, grounding you like roots in the earth,"

Sarah continued.

Lily pictured sturdy roots extending from her body into the ground, just like the Wise Tree, providing stability and strength.

Sarah whispered,

> "with each breath, allow the ancient wisdom of the Wise Tree to flow into you, anchoring and calming you."

Lily envisioned the tree's tranquility and resilience flowing into her with each inhale. Her mind became as still and clear as a glassy forest pond.

> "Remember this sense of inner calm you've found here. You can revisit this place of peace whenever you feel worried or overwhelmed."

Lily smiled, knowing she could return to this serene inner sanctuary at any time. She followed her mother's guidance, breathing deeply and feeling a cocoon of tranquility envelop her.

When at last, they opened their eyes, Lily beamed with joy.

> "That was amazing, Mommy! I felt the Wise Tree speaking to me, sharing its wisdom."

Sarah smiled affectionately at her daughter.

> "I'm so glad you enjoyed it and were open to receiving the tree's teachings. Even when life gets difficult, you now know you can always find inner calm and strength."

As Lily and Sarah bid the Wise Tree farewell, they felt its energy lingering like a warm embrace. The tree had shown them the peace that comes from remaining rooted during adversity.

Whenever Lily felt stressed or anxious, she would picture the Wise Tree and sink into mindful breaths. The tree's resilience became a source of comfort and wisdom for her.

Many years later, an adult Lily returned to the forest with her own child to meet the ancient Wise Tree. Just like her mother had once guided her, Lily now shared the tree's teachings about finding inner calm amidst life's storms.

The Wise Tree's branches stretched high into the sky, having weathered the seasons. But its timeless message remained for generations to come - true wisdom comes from within.

The end.

"THE ODYSSEY OF THE MINDFUL VOYAGER"
STORYTIME:

© 2023 Manon Doucet. All rights reserved.

The Mindful Adventure of Andrew and Mom

One sunny morning, rays of light filtered through the bedroom window curtains, landing softly on young Andrew's resting face. He scrunched his eyes and nose as the brightness stirred him awake. Once he adjusted to the morning glow, Andrew's senses came alive. He smelled the sweet aroma of waffles wafting from the kitchen downstairs and heard the comforting clatter of dishes being stacked.

Andrew's mother, Rachel, was already up preparing a surprise breakfast-in-bed for her son's big day. Today was his 7th birthday, and she wanted it to be extra special.

> "Good morning, birthday boy!"

Rachel cheerfully greeted Andrew as he bounded down the stairs.

> "I made your favorite for breakfast - waffles with strawberries and whipped cream!"

Andrew's eyes widened with delight.

> "Wow, thanks, Mom! This looks awesome."

He said, licking his lips excitedly.
After enjoying the tasty meal together, Rachel had a surprise up her sleeve.

> "I was thinking, how would you like to go on a special adventure today to celebrate your birthday?"

She asked, a playful twinkle in her eye.

> "A birthday adventure?! Yes, please!"

Andrew exclaimed, nearly knocking over his orange juice in enthusiasm.

Rachel chuckled at her son's reaction.

> "I had a feeling you'd be on board."

She said, ruffling his sandy blonde hair.

> "But this won't be just any old adventure. Today, we're going to be mindful explorers!"

Andrew looked at his mom curiously.

> "Mindful explorers? What does that mean?"

> "I'm so glad you asked!"

said Rachel.

> "Being a mindful explorer means observing our surroundings closely, using all our senses. It means being fully present in each moment as we discover new things."

Rachel could see the wheels turning in Andrew's head as he processed the idea. She knew her son loved examining the world around him with great curiosity.

> "That sounds awesome!"

Andrew finally proclaimed.

> "I'm ready to be a mindful explorer, Mom!"

> "Wonderful!"

Said Rachel, smiling.

> "This will be a birthday you'll never forget."

And so their mindful expedition began, starting with a leisurely stroll through the lush green forest near their home. As they walked along the twisting dirt path surrounded by soaring pines, Rachel guided her son.

> "As we walk, notice how the fresh morning air feels against your skin. Breathe it in deeply through your nose. What do you smell?"

she asked.

Andrew shut his eyes and inhaled slowly, taking in the woodsy scents.

> "It's crisp and earthy, like the forest after a rainstorm."

He remarked after a moment.
Rachel nodded approvingly.

> "You're absolutely right. By paying such close attention, we appreciate things we normally overlook."

Their meandering path soon led to an open meadow filled with flowers swaying gently in the breeze. Vibrant yellows, purples, pinks, and oranges dotted the grassy landscape.

> "Feel the soft grass under your bare feet."

Instructed Rachel, as Andrew had insisted on removing his sneakers.

> "Can you sense the warmth of the sun on your skin?"

Andrew wiggled his toes, tickled by the grass blades. He turned his face upward, letting the sun's rays wash over him.

> "Mmm hmm, it feels so nice and cozy, like a big hug!"

He told his mom.

> "Remain aware of that warmth inside and out,"

said, Rachel.

> "Mindfulness helps us find stability from within."

She gave him a loving squeeze, just as a passing butterfly with mosaic wings alighted on a nearby blossom.

> "Wow, look, Mom!"

Exclaimed Andrew. Rachel was happy to see his sense of childlike wonder so alive.

The mindful adventurers carried on, eventually coming upon a flowing stream surrounded by mossy stones. The clear water danced and sparkled as it tripped over the rocks.

> "Observe how the stream moves steadily forward, never rushing or lingering behind."

Instructed Rachel.

> "Let's try to live in this moment, like the water."

They sat together on the grass, watching the water appreciatively. Andrew grinned as a small fish swam into view, then darted beneath a rock.

> "The stream takes each moment as it comes."

Andrew remarked insightfully.

> "I want to live that way too - fully in the now."

Rachel's heart swelled with pride in her thoughtful son.

After a peaceful time streamside, their journey led them out of the secluded forest and into the neighboring bustling town. Rachel could sense Andrew growing a bit overwhelmed by all the honking cars, chatting pedestrians, barking dogs, and humming traffic lights.

> "I know there's a lot going on, but try this mindfulness technique called anchoring."

Rachel suggested gently.

> "Tune into the sensation of your feet touching the sidewalk. This can help provide stability when things feel hectic externally."

Andrew nodded, focusing on the solid pavement underneath his sneakers. He felt his racing mind start to steady as he directed his attention to the rise and fall of his feet.

Rachel smiled down at Andrew, knowing he had already picked up effective mindfulness skills to center himself. She gave his hand an encouraging squeeze.

Soon, they left the crowded downtown streets and wandered into a local park. As they strolled along a trail edged with vibrant wildflowers, Rachel said,

> "Now observe something in nature closely with all your senses. Appreciate all its tiny details and just be with it fully."

Andrew's eyes landed on a tiny ladybug crawling slowly up a plant stem. He crouched down and watched, transfixed, as the small insect wiggled its delicate legs and fluttered its spotted wings.

Studying just this one living thing so intently made Andrew feel profoundly connected to the natural world around him.

> "By paying attention with childlike curiosity, we see magic in the ordinary."

Remarked Rachel. Andrew's eyes shone as he took in her words along with the ladybug's every tiny movement.

As the day went on, Andrew and Rachel's birthday adventure led them to new neighborhoods and terrains, each providing opportunities for mindfulness and closer connection. They identified birds by their songs, felt the gritty roughness of tree bark, and observed their thoughts float by like clouds.

Eventually, their wanderings brought them to the base of a wooded hill. Rachel could tell Andrew was getting tired.

> "How about we rest for a bit?"

She suggested, pointing out a trail leading up the hill.

Andrew nodded, and they began trekking up the path as the ground sloped steadily upward beneath their feet. At the top, they reached an overlook with panoramic views of the valley below. Lush green forests and farmland unfurled below them like a grand tapestry. The silver thread of a river glittered in the distance.

Sitting atop a smooth boulder, Rachel said,

> "Take a moment to reflect. For what are you most grateful right now in this present moment?"

Andrew paused, gazing out at the commanding view.

> "Well, I'm really grateful for getting to have this awesome adventure with you today, Mom. And also for feeling so peaceful and happy inside my heart."

Rachel wrapped her arms around her thoughtful son, choked up by his profound words. At only seven years old, he had already discovered so much about mindfulness and presence.

As the sun dipped lower in the sky, ending their magical mindful tour, Andrew gave his mom a big birthday hug.

> "Thank you for the best birthday ever!"

He told her.

> "I loved exploring the world in this more mindful way."

Rachel kissed the top of her son's head.

> "Keep nurturing your sense of mindfulness, my dear. Curiosity, attention, and open-heartedness will serve you well wherever you go in life."

Andrew nodded, knowing he would remember and treasure this special journey for many mindful moments to come.

As Rachel tucked Andrew into bed that night, she watched his eyes flutter closed, his mind at ease. Her greatest birthday wish was for her son to grow up with wonder, wisdom, and inner peace. Their mindful adventure that day had set him on the right path.

The End.

"THE MAGIC BREATH"
STORYTIME:

© 2023 Foss Plus. All rights reserved.

"The Magic Breath"

Once upon a time, in a world where magic lived in every corner, there was a young and inquisitive fairy named Bella. She delighted in exploring the depths of the enchanted forest, discovering new wonders around each tree and under every stone.

    One sunny morning, as Bella fluttered and zipped among the

wildflowers, she noticed a wise old owl perched on a mossy branch above her. His large amber eyes blinked down at the petite fairy as he spoke in a calm, knowing voice.

> "Hoo-hoo, little one. Have you heard about the magic hidden inside your very breath?"

Bella paused, her fluttering wings suspended mid-air in surprise. She gazed up at the learned owl, intrigued.

> "Magic of my breath, you say? No, I haven't, Mr. Owl! What do you mean?"

She asked eagerly, drifting closer to him.
The owl gave a gentle hoot.

> "Your breath holds a power you've yet to discover, young one. When you pay close attention to each inhale and exhale, your breath can soothe your mind and calm your spirit."

Bella's eyes grew wide with wonder. She settled on top of a mushroom near the owl's perch, eager to unlock the secrets of this magic.

> "Teach me, wise owl! I want to learn,"

she implored.

> "Very well."

Replied the owl.

> "Let's begin with a simple breathing exercise. Close your eyes, focus on your breath, and breathe in slowly and deeply through your nose as if smelling a delicious morning dew."

Eager to awaken the power within, Bella closed her eyes and inhaled slowly and deeply. In her mind, she imagined breathing in the fresh, sweet scent of morning grass.

> "Good, good. Now gently release the breath through your mouth, like a soft breeze through the trees."

Instructed the owl

Bella exhaled steadily, envisioning her breath as a whispered wind weaving through the forest. Immediately she felt a sense of peace and calm enveloped her.

Eyes still closed, she said,

> "Oh, wow! I can feel it working. My mind feels so serene."

"You see?"

Replied the owl.

> "Your breath can be a valuable tool to find tranquility amidst life's storms. With practice, it becomes a magical anchor you can return to anytime."

From that day on, Bella practiced her magic breath daily. When faced with difficult emotions, stressful events, or fearful situations, she would close her eyes, focus on her breath, and inhale and exhale deeply. And without fail, this ritual returned her to a place of peace and clarity.

One morning, while sipping dewdrops with her best fairy friends, Lily and Oliver, Bella decided to share her discovery.

> "I want to show you both something magical."

She said. Lily and Oliver's eyes lit up.

> "Oooh, magic? We love magic!"

exclaimed Lily.

> "What mystical powers will we learn today?"

Bella smiled.

> "It's a power we already have within us. Let's fly to the rainbow grove, and I'll explain everything."

Soon they were seated comfortably atop a giant mushroom beneath dazzling rainbows arcing overhead.

> "So this magical power comes from...our breath?"

Asked Oliver, intrigued but skeptical.
Bella nodded eagerly.

> "Yes! All we must do is focus on slowly breathing in and out. Like this..."

She demonstrated her tranquil inhales and exhales.
Lily and Oliver exchanged amazed glances. Then Lily said,

> "It sounds so simple! Let's all try it together."

The three friends closed their eyes and followed Bella's guidance, inhaling deeply through their noses, envisioning breathing in peace and calm. Then they released the breaths slowly out through their mouths, visualizing any worries or fears drifting away.

A serene silence settled over the grove. After several minutes, Bella whispered,

> "How do you both feel?"

Lily and Oliver opened their eyes, faces glowing.

> "I feel so relaxed like I'm floating on a soft cloud!"

Said Lily dreamily.

> "Me too,"

Oliver agreed.

> "It's like I can leave all troubles far behind just by focusing on my breath."

Bella's heart swelled.

> "I'm so glad you can feel its powers too! We all have access to this magic inside us anytime we need relief or comfort."

From then on, the three fairies practiced their magic breaths together when facing difficult times. And without fail, these tranquil breaths united and centered them, reminding them of the peace within.

One day, Oliver became frightened when a storm rolled across the forest, shaking the trees ferociously. Thunder crashed, and rain pounded the flower petals.

> "Help, I'm scared!"

Oliver cried, shivering beneath a leaf. But then he remembered his magic breath. He inhaled and exhaled deeply, finding solace in the breaths' soothing rhythm. Soon his trembling ceased, and calm returned.

When Lily lost a possession she cherished, distraught tears filled her eyes. But a few magic breaths later, she regained perspective and hope.

And whenever Bella felt overwhelmed or anxious, her magic breath never failed to guide her back to tranquility.

The fairies soon realized their breath's power extended beyond just helping themselves. Their slow, deliberate exhales could spread calmness to others around them too.

One evening, Bella and Lily noticed a firefly friend looking forlorn. His usually bright glow had dimmed with sadness. Bella had an idea. She and Lily slowly demonstrated their magic breaths, inhaling serenity and exhaling compassion. Before long, the firefly's glow returned, cheered by their mindful presence.

Another day, Oliver came across a young squirrel crying, its small paw stuck in a tree hollow. Oliver calmly breathed in and out, sending waves of tranquility to the frightened squirrel. As if sensing the soothing energy, the squirrel ceased its struggles, allowing Oliver to gently free its paw.

The three fairies' wise old owl mentor looked on proudly as they spread this breath magic throughout the forest.

"You see, young ones?"

he said.

"The gift of breath you share so selflessly brings more light and peace wherever you fly."

And so, even long after they were grown, Bella, Lily, and Oliver continued breathing magic into the world. Their tranquil breaths served as beacons of light during dark times and reminders of the peace within. They had learned life's greatest wisdom: the power they sought had been inside them all along.

The end.

"THE RAINBOW OF EMOTIONS"
STORYTIME:

© 2023 Foss Plus. All rights reserved.

"The Rainbow of Emotions"

Once upon a time, in a world of vibrant hues, there existed a magical rainbow that held the key to understanding our emotions. This was no ordinary rainbow but rather one that shimmered with all the colors of human feelings.

One sunny day, a curious young girl named Evelyn wandered into a wildflower meadow. Looking up, she spotted a dazzling rainbow arcing overhead. As Evelyn gazed in awe, a friendly voice suddenly spoke.

> "Hello there! I'm the Rainbow of Emotions."

Evelyn jumped, eyes wide.

> "You can talk?"

She asked incredulously.
The rainbow chuckled, colors rippling.

> "Why yes, though only to those willing to listen. And you, my dear, have an open mind and compassionate heart."

Evelyn blushed at the praise.

> "What do you mean you're the Rainbow of Emotions?"

she inquired.

> "Ah, insightful question!"

Replied the rainbow.

> "Each of my colors represents a different feeling. Like a spectrum, I contain the full array of human emotions."

> "Can you show me?"

Evelyn asked eagerly.

"With pleasure."

Said the rainbow.

"To start, what color do you think symbolizes happiness?"

Evelyn pondered a moment.

"Yellow, like sunshine!"

she declared.

"Correct!"

The rainbow glowed a vibrant yellow.

"When you feel cheerful and joyful, embrace your inner sunshine!"

"Now, what color resonates with calmness to you?"

Continued the rainbow.
Evelyn thought hard.

"Blue, like a peaceful sky."

She finally said.

"Wonderful!"

Soothing azure rippled through the rainbow.

> "Remember blue's tranquility during stressful times."

> "Let's keep going!"

Said the rainbow enthusiastically.

> "What color embodies anger for you?"

> "Red, like fire!"

Responded Evelyn without hesitation.

> "Precisely."

The rainbow burned crimson for a moment before returning to equilibrium.

> "Red often signals unchecked emotions. Mindfulness can restore balance."

> "How about sadness?"

The rainbow gently asked next.

> "Hmm...purple."

Said Evelyn thoughtfully.

> "It's often gloomy and lonely."

The rainbow shifted to a dull lavender.

> "Yes, but in sadness, we can also find wisdom and growth."

Evelyn's eyes shone with curiosity.

> "Can we do more?"

she pleaded.

The rainbow was delighted to continue. Soon, Evelyn correctly identified orange with joy, pink with love, green with peacefulness, and more. Each color transformation reinforced Emotion's lessons.

> "You're a fast learner!"

Praised the rainbow finally.

Evelyn smiled, basking in the glow of colors and knowledge. But she desired more.

> "Could we meditate together on the emotions?"

She asked hopefully.

> "A wonderful idea."

Said the rainbow.

> "Make yourself comfortable."

Evelyn settled cross-legged into the sweet meadow grass. The rainbow dimmed to a tranquil hue and began guiding her through a visualization.

> "Close your eyes and take some centering breaths."

Came the calm voice. Evelyn felt any tension melt away with each exhale.

> "Picture yourself standing before me, the Rainbow of Emotions."

Continued the rainbow. In her mind's eye, Evelyn saw its vivid colors shimmering.

> "As you breathe deeply now, allow each color to envelop you, one emotion at a time."

Instructed the rainbow.

Evelyn envisioned a warm yellow light filled with joy and laughter. It started in her heart, spilling out until she was basked in its glow.

Next floated in serene blue, bringing a sense of inner peace and tranquility. Then fiery red ignited her senses for a flash, a flare of power quickly cooling to resolve.

One by one, each color swirled gently through her body and mind. Evelyn observed their ephemeral nature, arriving in waves, then drifting away like clouds.

By the meditation's end, Evelyn felt centered, with deeper compassion for each emotion's message. As she opened her eyes, the rainbow's aura seemed to nuzzle her affectionately.

> "How was that, my dear?"

it asked.

> "Amazing!"

breathed Evelyn.

> "It felt like a journey through my own feelings. I understand them better now."

The rainbow glowed with pride at having guided this child's self-discovery.

> "Remember, emotions are ever-changing guests."

It told her.

> "Welcome them, learn from them, then watch them move on."

Evelyn promised she would. She now saw her feelings as teachers, not tyrants. With the rainbow's guidance, she had found a bridge to inner wisdom.

From then on, the rainbow remained Evelyn's trusted confidant and counselor as she navigated life's emotional currents and storms. When rage, sorrow, or fear threatened to overwhelm her, it taught her to pause, breathe, and observe with compassion.

The rainbow reminded Evelyn that no emotion lasts forever, though their lessons do. Each one added richness and color to the meaning of being human.

Years later, when Evelyn had children of her own, she shared the Rainbow of Emotions with them. Together, they identified thoughts and feelings by color, embraced them, then watched them drift away like clouds.

One dark night, Evelyn was awakened by her anxious daughter crawling into bed with her, frightened by a nightmare. As they sat cradled together, Evelyn pointed to the window.

Though it was dark outside, through the glass shone the faint arc of a familiar rainbow. Its mere presence soothed her daughter's fears.

Evelyn smiled, remembering the magical rainbow from childhood that had introduced her to the complex landscape of emotions. It had lit a path she still followed, encouraged by that wisdom from within.

Gazing at the ephemeral rainbow with her daughter nestled close, Evelyn felt blessed by this legacy of light she had received and could now pass on. Its vivid lessons would continue on, shining through many generations to come.

The end.

"THE GRATITUDE GARDEN"
STORYTIME:

© 2023 Manon Doucet. All rights reserved.

"The Gratitude Garden"

Once upon a time, in a land brimming with natural wonder, there existed an enchanted place called the Gratitude Garden. This mystical garden overflowed with radiant flowers in every vivid hue, all nurtured by the power of gratitude.

One sunny spring morning, a curious young girl named Lily set off down a winding forest path with her mother and father by her side. Birds trilled overhead as dappled sunlight filtered through the leafy canopy. The rich scent of blooming wildflowers perfumed the air.

> "Where are we going today?"

Lily inquired, skipping along happily and clutching a small hand-drawn map.

Lily's mother smiled down at her.

> "Somewhere very special - the Gratitude Garden!"

> "What's that?"

Lily asked, her eyes lighting up.

> "It's a magical garden where we can plant seeds of gratitude,"

Lily's father explained.

> "By focusing on what we're thankful for, those good things will blossom even more."

Enchanted by this idea, Lily eagerly hurried her steps. Before long, the forest opened up to reveal a sunny clearing. Colorful blooms carpeted the meadow, and a carved wooden archway welcomed them to 'The Gratitude Garden."

> "It's gorgeous!"

gasped Lily, turning in place to admire the flowers. The petals seemed to glow from an inner light. Her skin tingled with the garden's warm, hopeful energy.

> "This is a wonderful place to practice gratitude,"

said Lily's mother.

> "Let's find a quiet spot to meditate."

They settled onto soft grass near a babbling creek. Lily sat cross-legged, ready for her lesson.

With soothing voices, her parents guided her to relax and close her eyes.

> "Picture in your mind a packet of magical gratitude seeds,"

her father instructed.

Lily envisioned a colorful bundle of seeds cradled in her palms, each one shimmering slightly.

> "Now, what are you grateful for?"

her mother gently prompted.

> "As you think of something, take a deep breath in. And as you exhale, imagine planting one of your special seeds."

Lily contemplated all the gifts life had brought her.

> "I'm grateful for my cozy bed!"

She inhaled deeply as if breathing in joy itself. On her exhale, she envisioned nestling a glowing seed into the rich soil.

> "I'm grateful for playgrounds and my friends!"

Another inhalation of gratitude, another seed of thankfulness planted.

Lily and her parents continued the practice, cultivating a garden of appreciation within their hearts and minds. They planted vibrant seeds representing friends, family, warm meals, sunshine, trees, music, and more.

With each expression of gratitude, Lily felt her spirit lighten as if she had released a burden. Her insides seemed to grow brighter, like flowers turning toward the sun.

After the meditation, Lily blinked her eyes open. The physical garden now seemed to glow with a deeper luster. Its beauty reflected the inner joy Lily felt as she focused on life's gifts.

"That was wonderful,"

Lily whispered, embracing her parents.

"I can't wait to come back and plant more!"

They bid farewell to the tranquil grove. Within Lily, a wellspring of gratitude now bubbled as the seeds she had planted took root.

True to her word, Lily visited the garden often to nurture her gratitude practice. Whenever she became upset, frustrated, or discouraged, she would close her eyes, take a deep breath, and venture back to the Gratitude Garden in her mind's eye.

She imagined wandering through the vibrant blooms and fertile soil, planting seeds of thankfulness for friendship, family, health, and more. The exercise never failed to lift her spirits and bring her focus back to life's blessings.

Over time, Lily found that visiting her secret gratitude garden had the power to not only shift her own mood but also brighten the lives of those around her.

On days when her mother seemed weary or worried, Lily would gently take her hand and guide her through a gratitude meditation. The creases in her mother's forehead would soften as she followed Lily's lead.

When Lily's best friend was upset about moving away, they sat together, eyes closed, voicing thankful thoughts and imagining planting them in the earth like seeds. Her friend seemed comforted, knowing they shared this inner source of hope.

Though life brought inevitable sorrows and storms, Lily's Gratitude Garden remained a place of light she could always retreat to. It helped transform struggles into opportunities to recognize the gifts that remained.

Many years later, Lily walked through the familiar forest, now accompanied by her own young daughter. When they arrived at the clearing, Lily was delighted to see the wooden Gratitude Garden archway just as she remembered.

Her daughter's eyes widened at the sight of the dazzling meadow.

"It's magical!"

she gasped.

Lily smiled, knowing the real magic lived in their hearts. Taking her daughter's hand, she stepped joyfully into the garden.

"Are you ready to plant some beautiful seeds?"

Lily asked.

Her daughter nodded eagerly. Lily guided her to sit among the wildflowers as bees murmured lazily.

Together, they closed their eyes and began planting seeds of gratitude - starting the next generation on a garden that would continue to bloom for years to come.

The end.

"THE ANTS"
STORYTIME:

© 2023 Foss Plus. All rights reserved.

"The Ants"

Once upon a time, in a sprawling garden filled with vibrant flowers and grass stalks swaying like trees, there bustled a busy community of tiny ants. These ants were special, for they knew secrets of mindfulness that allowed them to live each moment fully.

One sunny morning, a young boy named Andrew sat cross-legged beneath a sturdy oak tree with his father at his side. Sweet floral scents drifted on the soft breeze as bees droned lazily among the blossoms.

Andrew's father turned to him with a playful glint in his eye.

> "I have an idea for a fun adventure today. Let's imagine we've shrunk down to the size of ants! We'll explore this garden world from their perspective."

Andrew's face lit up at the thought.

> "Wow, being tiny ants? That sounds awesome!"

His mind raced, imagining life down in the grass.

> "Alright, let's begin our meditation by closing our eyes and taking a few deep, centering breaths."

His dad instructed. Andrew focused on his inhale and exhale, feeling his body relax.

> "Now, picture yourself gradually shrinking down, down, down...getting tinier and tinier..."

Said his dad in a lulling tone.

Andrew envisioned the world expanding around him as he shrank smaller and smaller until he was no bigger than an ant!

> "Open your eyes slowly."

Guided his father.

"Welcome to the world of ants!"

Andrew opened his eyes and gasped. The blades of grass towered like stately pine trees. Flowers loomed like massive mountains. The garden seemed endless in every direction. A thrill of awe tingled through him.

"This is amazing!"

Breathed Andrew. Together, he and his dad began crawling on hands and knees down a winding earthen path between the grass stalks. The sun's warmth felt cozy on their backs.

As they crawled along, the mundane thoughts of Andrew's human-sized life came back - what games he would play later, what was for lunch. Suddenly, a broad leaf floated down and landed right in his path, blocking the way.

Andrew blinked in surprise.

"Whoa, now there's a leaf in my way! I guess my mind got distracted."

His dad nodded thoughtfully.

"Yes, that falling leaf can represent anything that pulls us out of the present moment. It's a gentle reminder to refocus on where we are."

Andrew examined the veined leaf, still in awe of how huge it seemed. Then he continued forward, keeping his senses tuned to the ant world around him. He listened to birdsong echoing from far above and smelled the sweet pollen dusting the air.

Further along, another leaf fell in front of Andrew's dad, causing him to pause.

> "It seems my mind also drifted away."

He remarked.

> "Let's refocus together."

They crawled onward, taking time to appreciate the small wonders all around them - a ladybug lumbering past, a droplet of dew shimmering on a blade of grass. More leaves fell when thoughts intruded, but they simply provided a redirect back to mindful presence.

At last, it was time to return from the ant's world. Settling once more beneath the old oak, Andrew opened his eyes, full-size again. He turned to his dad with an awed smile.

> "That was so cool! It made me really pay attention to everything around me."

Said Andrew.

> "Those falling leaves kept me in the moment."

His father drew him in for a proud hug.

> "You learned so well how we can immerse ourselves in the present. Remember this feeling as you go through each day."

Andrew nodded, knowing he had been gifted a joyful new perspective to carry with him. He felt deeply grateful for this precious time with his dad and the garden's gentle teachings.

In the days that followed, whenever Andrew felt stressed or distracted, he would close his eyes and picture himself back in the bustling garden as a mindful ant. He would imagine reacting calmly when leaves fell across his path, never losing focus.

Over time, Andrew found he could call upon this visualization anytime he needed to recenter himself in the present. It allowed him to approach his days with more patience, curiosity, and awe.

The garden **'ant'** meditation also affected how Andrew related to others. He tried to give his full attention when friends shared problems with him. His eyes followed passing birds now, whereas before, he may have tuned them out. The world seemed vibrant and alive.

Years later, Andrew became a father himself. He cherished the memory of that special day pretending to be tiny ants with his own dad. Now, with his young son, they crawled through grass-blade forests, observed colorful flower mountains, and found focus when leaves fell.

And so the garden lived on, not just in reality but in the minds and hearts of those who played within it. Each time they visited its contemplative paths, they recommitted to living each moment as fully as the ants.

Andrew learned that mindfulness lives all around us, in tiny details and quiet moments. We need only the willingness to shrink our perspective now and then to find life's hidden depth and poetry. A whole world waits there.

The end.

"THE FAMILY GARDEN"
STORYTIME:

© 2023 Foss Plus. All rights reserved.

"The Family Garden"

Once upon a time, in a cozy house with a sprawling backyard, there lived a loving family of four - The parents, Manon and Kevin, older sister Laurie, and the littlest one, Nerys. They were a family who cherished nature and wanted to create something beautiful together.

One sunny spring morning, as birdsongs filled the air, Manon and Kevin gathered their daughters with an exciting idea.

> "How would you girls like to help us build a family garden?"

Kevin asked, smiling at their eager faces.

> "Yes, yes, yes!"

Cheered Nerys, nearly dropping her stuffed bunny in enthusiasm.

Laurie grinned.

> "That sounds so fun! When can we start?"

Manon laughed affectionately at her daughters' reactions.

> "Right away! We've got the perfect little plot ready to be planted."

The family headed out to the backyard hand-in-hand, where a section had been prepared with rich, fertile soil. Manon and Kevin had even marked it with colorful stones reading

"Our Family Garden."

Kevin handed Laurie a packet of seeds.

> "Here are your flower seeds, Laurie. You'll be in charge of planting them."

Laurie accepted them reverently, admiring the delicate shapes. She knelt and pressed each seed into the dirt with care, imagining the vibrant blooms to come.

Meanwhile, little Nerys was given the very important job of watering the garden. Kevin handed her a miniature watering can.

> "Remember to give each new seed a refreshing drink."

He told her.

Nerys tipped the can over each seedling, watching the drops darken the soil. She felt connected to the tiny sprouts, helping nourish their growth.

Soon, the whole family was hard at work preparing the budding garden. Manon gently raked the soil while Kevin uprooted weeds. Together, they sculpted the landscape with mindfulness.

As they worked, Manon reminded the girls to engage all their senses.

> "Laurie, notice how the rich soil feels between your fingers. Nerys, listen to the cheerful robins singing."

The girls slowed down, absorbing the textures, smells, tastes, and sounds around them. Nerys paused to feel the sun's warmth soaking into her skin. Laurie traced the intricate veins of a leaf. Their parents smiled, cultivating this mindful engagement in their daughters.

After preparing the plot, everyone gathered for a soothing garden meditation. Settling onto the soft grass, they shut their eyes and focused on their breath, inhaling the earthy scents.

> "Picture the sprouts growing day by day, reaching for the sun."

Manon guided in a hushed tone. The girls envisioned tiny seedlings bursting through the soil, leaves unfurling, and stems steadily rising. They imagined budding flowers, busy bees, and ripe vegetables to share.

Kevin led them in cultivating gratitude next.

> "For what are we most thankful about our family garden?"

He asked.

Nerys piped up instantly,

> "I'm grateful we're planting it together!"

> "I'm thankful for getting to see nature's beauty up close."

Laurie added thoughtfully. The parents squeezed each other's hands, moved by their daughters' wisdom.

Over the next weeks, the family nurtured their garden with care and mindfulness. They inspected for aphids, added fertilizer, and built a little fence to keep out nibbling bunnies. Every day brought new delights - the first tomato ripening, carrots poking up from the soil, and zinnias opening their petals.

On lazy evenings, the family sat amidst the garden, observing their efforts flourish around them. The girls would excitedly point out each new bud and blossom.

One night, as the sun set orange and pink behind the swaying sunflowers, Manon remarked,

> "This garden has grown into so much more than just plants and blooms. It's our shared space of togetherness."

> "And mindfulness!"

Nerys piped in, remembering their meditation.

> "That's right,"

Kevin said, hugging her.

> "This garden will feed our bodies, but also our souls."

Laurie nodded thoughtfully, already feeling the garden sewing their family closer together through the seasons.

At summer's end, they harvested baskets full of plump tomatoes, aromatic basil, and flowers for bouquets. Over dinner al fresco in the garden, they adorned their meals with the literal fruits of their labor.

In the years to come, even as the girls grew up, the garden remained their cherished sanctuary where they returned to remember what mattered - nurturing life and each other.

They would walk between the pea trellises and berry bushes, now tall and strong like the sisters themselves. The girls would brush their fingers over the faded stone markers -

> "OUR FAMILY GARDEN"

- and take a quiet moment to feel six years old again.

One spring morning, Laurie wandered through with her baby boy.

> "This is our family garden."

She whispered to him as they sat among the lilies.

> "We'll plant new seeds together here soon."

And so the garden lived on, its roots reaching as deep as the family's bonds. It became their legacy of mindfulness, nourishment, and time together - the space where they grew.

The end.

"THE MINDFUL EXPLORER"
STORYTIME:

© 2023 Foss Plus. All rights reserved.

"The Mindful Explorer"

Once upon a time, nestled between soaring mountains and a glittering river, there lay a charming little town. And in this idyllic haven lived a young boy named Jason, who cherished adventure and possessed an imagination that could ignite even the most mundane moment into something magical.

Each sunny day after school, Jason would set out to explore his surroundings, seeking hidden wonders that only he could unveil. On this particular afternoon, Jason slung on his trusty binoculars and donned his wide-brimmed explorer's hat. He was especially eager to discover new surprises on this auspicious day.

Stepping out into the backyard, which to Jason seemed an endless jungle of mysteries, he took a deep breath of anticipation.

> "Today"

he declared,

> "I will be The Mindful Explorer!"

Jason began his expedition, moving slowly and deliberately through the yard. He felt the spongy grass beneath his shoes and tilted his face skyward to enjoy the breeze. With eyes closed, Jason tuned in to the lively bird songs and rustling leaves composing nature's symphony.

When he blinked his eyes open again, Jason decided his first mission would be befriending a small black ant crawling across his path. Crouching down, Jason watched the ant intently before speaking to it in a hushed, polite voice.

> "Hello there, Mr. Ant. Where are you off to today?"

To Jason's astonishment, the ant looked up and replied,

> "Why, I'm gathering food for my colony! Busy days ahead, busy days!"

Antes busily scurried on his way.

Jason's eyes shone with wonder.

> "Thank you for showing me how even the smallest creatures have big, important jobs to do."

He said. The ant gave a friendly wave of his antennae before disappearing into the grass.

Continuing on, Jason discovered a sparkling stone nestled in the dirt. He held it up to the light, enthralled by the way the sun's rays refracted off its surface into miniature rainbows.

> "I'm grateful for the beauty offered by the simplest of things,"

Jason thought. This was a treasure he would definitely add to his collection.

As Jason roamed deeper into the yard, the sun's angle shifted to late afternoon. Before him lay a patch of brilliant wildflowers, their faces upturned toward the fading light. Jason shut his eyes and inhaled their perfume - sweet tinges of lavender and rose mingling with grassy undertones.

Opening his eyes, Jason gazed at the flowers and allowed their luminescent colors to fill his senses.

> "Nature's stained glass."

He proclaimed with quiet reverence.

With each new discovery on Jason's meandering path, he felt more in tune with the natural world. His explorer's mind buzzed with curiosity about the tiniest details, like sunlight dancing on a leaf or the feel of bark beneath his hand. Jason found joy in the present, just as it was, without wishing for more.

As the sun dipped below the horizon, Jason found a grassy spot beneath a sturdy oak to rest and reflect on the day's adventures. He felt the ridges of bark against his back and studied the intricate patterns of leaves forming a canopy high above.

"Thank you, tall oak, for your steady presence and shelter,"

Jason whispered, overcome with gratitude for all he had experienced. He had discovered boundless treasures, not in far-off places, but simply by opening his eyes and heart to the wonders of the present.

That night, tucked beneath his covers, Jason's mind replayed each moment of his journey in vivid color - the shimmering stone, the wildflowers' sweet perfume, the wise old oak. Falling asleep, he felt both centered and open to possibility.

From then on, Jason carried the spirit of The Mindful Explorer with him wherever he went. On lazy Sundays, he wandered his backyard with creativity and curiosity, uncovering endless magic. Even on school days, he practiced mindfulness by pausing to observe a fluttering leaf or to thank the clouds for their funny shapes.

In time, others also noticed the aura of appreciation Jason carried with him. His friends began pointing out wonders they might have overlooked before, from the patterns of a spider web to the colors of sidewalk chalk. Bit by bit, Jason's mindfulness rippled out into the world beyond him.

Though the years carried Jason far beyond the haven of his childhood backyard, he never lost touch with his inner explorer. As an adult, Jason became a devoted husband and father. But he still set aside mindful time to meander and appreciate life's simple treasures with his own children.

And thanks to one especially imaginative boy named Jason, who saw marvels within the ordinary, generations to come would have eyes opened to the secret wonders all around them, waiting only to be noticed.

The end.

PART 3: GUIDING PARENTS AND CAREGIVERS

Stories for Parents and Caregivers to Help Them with Their Children's Meditation
Games for Parents and Caregivers to Help Teach Meditation Techniques
Mindful Breathing and Other Exercises
Guided Meditation Exercises

CHAPTER 9
STORIES FOR PARENTS AND CAREGIVERS TO HELP THEM WITH THEIR CHILDREN'S MEDITATION
MAKING MEDITATION ENGAGING AND RELATABLE FOR CHILDREN

INTRODUCING children to the practice of meditation can seem daunting at first. Sitting still and tuning into the present moment may appear complex or unappealing to their young, active minds. However, with creativity and compassion, we can adapt meditation into engaging, child-friendly practices that speak to their hearts.

In this chapter, we explore strategies to make meditation more relatable and enjoyable for children. By infusing play, imagination, variety, and celebration into the process, meditation becomes an adventure rather than a chore. Our aim is to provide parents and caregivers with ideas and inspiration to meet children where they are developmentally and guide them happily on this journey of self-discovery.

MAKING IT PLAYFUL

Children learn best through play.

> According to childhood development expert "Play helps children develop creativity and imagination while building skills to handle stress and adversity." (Starko, 2021)
>
> Rather than traditional sitting meditation, parents can introduce mindfulness through playful activities children naturally enjoy. (Dupeyrat & Bernard, 2019)

Games like Follow the Leader, which incorporates mindful walking or activities like mindful coloring that involves fully focusing on the present sensory experience, integrate mindfulness without forcing children into a rigid practice. Having stuffed animals lead breathing or blowing bubbles slowly to inspire focused breaths turns meditation into a lively game.

Outdoor playtime also presents moments to pause and tune into nature's beauty just as it is - the flutter of birds, the feeling of grass underfoot, and the dance of trees in the wind. Leveraging existing play provides an easy on-ramp to practice being fully present.

The key is tapping into play's capacity to cultivate joy, curiosity, and engagement. When children associate meditation with playtime adventures rather than mandated stillness, they dive in willingly.

USING IMAGINATION

Children thrive when their imagination is activated.

> Fantasy lays the foundation for cognitive tools like symbolic thinking and creativity. (Paley, 2009)

Caregivers can spark kids' interest in meditation by introducing key concepts through imaginative stories and guided visualization.

For example, a story about traveling underwater to a magical kingdom helps children envision finding inner calm. They can imagine befriending a dolphin who teaches them about taking slow, steady breaths. By becoming part of an exciting storyline, children absorb lessons naturally.

Creative visualizations build upon children's innate imagination. One technique invites children to picture a secret garden with butterflies, using all their senses to explore its beauty. This engages them fully in the mindfulness exercise. Linking guided imagery to themes that fascinate children makes the practices more appealing.

Leveraging imagination and fantasy transforms meditation into a magical adventure rather than a didactic exercise. Children welcome inner discovery when it unfolds imaginatively.

OFFERING DIVERSE TECHNIQUES

Children have varying interests, strengths, and needs. Providing an array of meditation techniques allows them to find what resonates best.

"Like learning a language, each child will respond differently to different methods. Offering options like mindful movement, breathing exercises, or guided relaxation lets kids explore what works for them." (W. Stewart, 2017)

OPTIONS CAREGIVERS CAN PROVIDE INCLUDE:

Sensory meditation:

Focus on sounds, tastes, smells, and textures. Listen to birds, taste food slowly, and touch leaves.

Walking meditation:

Focus fully on the body's sensations during slow, conscious walking.

Breath awareness:

Follow each inhale/exhale, imagining the breath as a wave, balloon, or cloud.

Body scans:

Progressively relax each body part from toes to head. Release any tension.

Loving-kindness:
Send kind thoughts or prayers to yourself and others. Visualize them filled with light.

Gratitude:
Reflect on people, experiences, or qualities you feel grateful for to cultivate appreciation.

Trying a "tasting menu" of methods allows children to discover their favorites, just as offering various sports or crafts taps into diverse interests. Sample practices during family time, then allow children to select which they'd like to focus on. Providing options makes meditation more engaging.

KEEPING IT SHORT AND SWEET

Children tend to have shorter attention spans, so brief but frequent mindfulness practices work best.

> According to mindfulness educator Christopher Willard, sessions only need to be 1-3 minutes for toddlers, 5-7 minutes for ages 5-7, and 10-15 minutes for ages 10+ (Petts, 2019).

Shorter practices reduce restlessness and make meditation

more appealing.

It also helps to bookend longer practices with routines kids know. For example, starting after reading a story and ending by singing a song creates familiarity. Or follow active playtime with quiet meditation. Plotting sessions around existing patterns reinforces it as part of their schedule.

Weaving multiple very short practices into the day can be productive. Pausing to take mindful breaths before transitions or tuning into the senses during mundane tasks like eating or walking the dog builds the muscle of present-moment awareness over time without prolonged concentration.

Think snippets versus formal sittings. Brief moments spread consistently through the day, persistently planting the seeds of mindful attention.

MAKING IT SOCIAL

When introductory meditation is shared as a family activity, children often experience greater enjoyment.

> According to psychology professor Hooria Jazaieri:
> "Practicing mindfulness as a family strengthens interpersonal bonds while building individual skills. Children see that meditation matters when done together." (Cantor & Osher, 2021)

Dedicate 10 minutes after dinner when everyone participates in a guided breathing or gratitude practice. Let each family member take turns selecting a mindfulness activity the group will complete. Or go outside together, and each spends 1-2 minutes silently observing nature mindfully before sharing observations.

Group practice fosters a sense of belonging and normalizes mindfulness as a shared experience. It also provides built-in support, allowing parents to model mindfulness behaviors that children can mirror. Weaving it into family routines conveys its value.

CELEBRATING THE JOURNEY

Like any new skill, children may not take to meditation instantly. Parents can spark and sustain motivation by celebrating progress, offering incentives, and affirming effort.

Marking milestones like their first time sitting quietly for three whole minutes or completing a week of breath awareness builds pride in their development. Small rewards like choosing a family movie night after a week of practice positively reinforce behavior. Verbal praise for returning their attention during meditation acknowledges growth.

When children hit bumps, avoid criticism. Note missteps compassionately and reinforce that mindfulness takes practice. Remind them that every session builds their skills, even if progress feels slow. Affirming words and patience help children persist through challenges.

. . .

Soon, with consistent celebration and encouragement, meditation becomes its own reward as children come to appreciate its benefits. Each component - play, imagination, variety, brevity, community, and praise - transforms meditation into a rich and rewarding childhood adventure.

THE STORIES AND EXERCISES BELOW PROVIDE A GLIMPSE INTO MAKING MEDITATION CHILD-FRIENDLY:

The Butterfly Garden: A Mindful Adventure

Today, Leila and her brother Ayo decided to spend time in their special butterfly garden. As they sat comfortably on the grass, Leila noticed a blue butterfly with black stripes perched on a flower.

> "Watch it quietly with me,"

Whispered Leila.

> "Let's see what it does without disturbing it."

The children watched intently as the butterfly slowly flapped its wings up and down. Ayo smiled as the butterfly crawled to the edge of the petal. The children kept observing the butterfly with curiosity and wonder, enjoying this moment of mindfulness.

Leila and Ayo continued exploring the garden, noticing the different plants and insects around them. They quietly smelled fragrant flowers, felt the soft grass under their toes, and listened to birdsongs. Through their senses, the garden came alive with beauty.

. . .

At the end of their visit, Leila thought about how magical it was to pay full attention to their surroundings. She couldn't wait to practice mindfulness again in the colorful butterfly garden!

Reflection: When have you felt fully focused and present like Leila and Ayo? What did you notice around you?

MINDFUL MOVEMENT MEDITATION

Let's practice mindfulness through our bodies! Stand with your feet shoulder-width apart and imagine roots growing from your feet deep into the earth. As you inhale, grow tall like a tree reaching for sunlight. As you exhale, sway gently side to side like a tree in the wind.

Now, move slowly and mindfully through poses inspired by nature:
- Sway like seaweed underwater
- Bloom like a flower opening its petals
- Float like a leaf circling down to the ground

Notice how your body feels as you mindfully move and stretch. Bring your full attention to each graceful movement. Does your body feel energized or relaxed? By tuning into the present moment through mindful movement, you can cultivate awareness and enjoyment.

CHAPTER 10
GAMES FOR PARENTS AND CAREGIVERS TO HELP TEACH MEDITATION TECHNIQUES

THE INTRIGUING WORLD of mindfulness can seem distant and somewhat overwhelming when introduced to children. Yet, when interwoven with playful games and activities, mindfulness becomes an engaging and enjoyable endeavor. For parents and caregivers, it presents an opportunity to teach meditation techniques in a way that is accessible and inviting. These fun-filled activities can also become shared family experiences, enhancing bonding and mutual understanding.

In this chapter on meditation for children, parents, and caregivers, let's explore a variety of delightful and easy-to-play games that everyone can enjoy. These activities are just a starting point but don't feel restricted by them. Feel free to discover other games that your family will love, whether you play them individually or together. The key is to make the journey of meditation enjoyable and enriching for all!

1. MINDFUL SCAVENGER ADVENTURE: EXPLORE WITH YOUR SENSES!

Hey there, little adventurers! Are you ready for an exciting and mindful scavenger hunt? Get ready to embark on an amazing journey of experiential learning, where you'll explore the world around you using all your senses!

So, what's a mindful scavenger hunt all about? It's like a magical quest that transforms the familiar scavenger hunt game into a unique and mindful experience. You'll be presented with a list of special items or qualities to find in your immediate surroundings.

Here's the fun part – the items you'll be seeking aren't just any ordinary things! They're all about engaging with your senses. You might be on the lookout for something super soft, like the delicate touch of a flower petal. Or maybe, it's a splash of blue that catches your eye in the world around you.

But that's not all! This adventure is all about listening too. You might be prompted to tune in and listen carefully for the whisper of the wind as it rustles through the leaves.

Sounds cool, right? Well, here's the best part – this seemingly simple task becomes an amazing way to connect with the world mindfully. By using your senses to explore your surroundings, you'll fully immerse yourself in the joy of the present moment.

. . .

Oh, and guess what? This is a team effort! When you go on this scavenger adventure with your family, the excitement multiplies and the bonding experience becomes even more special.

So, let's get started on this incredible journey of mindful scavenging! Grab your list and let your senses guide you through the wonders of the world around you. Get ready to explore, learn, and have a whole lot of fun!

Are you up for the challenge, little explorers? Let the mindful scavenger adventure begin! Happy hunting! 🕵️🔍✨

2. BREATHING BUDDIES ADVENTURE: DISCOVER THE MAGIC OF MINDFUL BREATHING!

Hey there, little adventurers! Are you ready to embark on a magical journey called "Breathing Buddies"? It's a super simple yet enchanting game that will introduce you to the amazing world of breath awareness!

So, what's this fun game all about? Well, imagine having a special companion to join you on your mindful breathing adventure. It could be your favorite stuffed animal or a cute little toy – your very own "Breathing Buddy!"

Here's how the adventure unfolds – lie down comfortably, and place your Breathing Buddy on your belly. As you start to take slow, deep breaths, something magical happens – your buddy rises and falls, just like the rhythm of your breath!

. . .

It's like having a little friend to show you the way as you explore the wonders of mindful breathing. With each inhale and exhale, your buddy becomes a visual aid, helping you stay focused on the amazing process happening inside you.

And guess what? This game is not only fun but also super relaxing! You'll feel a sense of calm and tranquility wash over you as you connect with your breath and your buddy.

Do you know what's even cooler? Mindful breathing can sometimes seem like a big mystery, but with your Breathing Buddy by your side, it becomes clear and understandable, like magic!

Breathing Buddies is a wonderful way to start your journey into the world of mindfulness. It's like a secret potion that helps you relax, stay focused, and appreciate the magic of each breath.

So, are you ready to join the Breathing Buddies adventure? Grab your favorite stuffed animal or toy, lie down, and let the magic of mindful breathing unfold before your eyes!

Let your buddy be your guide as you dive into the fantastic world of breath awareness. Get ready to feel the calm, embrace the magic, and breathe in the wonders of this amazing game!

. . .

Happy Breathing Buddies adventure, little explorers!

3. MUSICAL MELODIES: JOURNEY INTO MINDFUL LISTENING!

Hey there, little music lovers! Get ready for a magical adventure called "Musical Mindfulness" – it's like a symphony of sound and awareness that will fill your heart with joy!

So, what's this amazing adventure all about? Well, it's all about using the power of music to help you become more mindful. Isn't that cool?

Here's how it works: parents and caregivers will play soft, calming music that will make you feel like you're floating on a cloud of melodies. As you listen carefully, you'll embark on a journey of mindful listening!

But wait, there's more! You'll get to play a fun game too – you might be asked to identify different instruments playing in the background. Is that the gentle strum of a guitar or the playful sound of a flute?

Or, you can pay attention to the rhythm and melody of the piece – it's like dancing to the music with your ears!

This exciting experience helps you fully engage in the wonderful world of sound. You'll be in tune with every note and beat, creating an environment perfect for mindful listening.

. . .

Oh, and here's a little secret – you can even close your eyes during this musical adventure! By doing so, you can dive deeper into the music, explore your thoughts and emotions, and feel a sense of calm and serenity inside you.

Musical Mindfulness is like a magical key that opens the door to your inner world. You'll discover the beauty of music and how it can make you feel calm and happy.

So, are you ready to set sail on this musical journey? Let the melodies guide you as you experience the wonder of mindful listening.

Get ready to embrace the magic of music and discover the joy of being fully present in the moment. It's time to let the musical melodies whisk you away on a mindful adventure like no other!

Happy listening, little music maestros! 🎵🎶🎧

4. JOYFUL JOURNEYS: EXPLORING MINDFUL MOVEMENT!

Hey there, little movers and shakers! Get ready to go on a fantastic journey of "Mindful Movement" – a magical way to connect with your body and have a whole lot of fun!

. . .

So, what's this exciting adventure all about? It's all about being aware of your body through gentle exercises like yoga or simple stretches. You'll be like graceful dancers, moving with mindfulness and joy!

Imagine this: as you do these exercises, you'll pay special attention to the rhythm of your breath. It's like a dance between your breath and your movements!

By doing this, you become a body awareness expert! You'll feel how your muscles stretch, the placement of your limbs, and even the incredible energy flowing within you!

But that's not all – this activity is like a superpower for your overall well-being! It makes you feel both physically and mentally strong and happy.

Mindful Movement is not just a regular exercise – it's like a playful way to become mindful in a hands-on, interactive manner. You get to feel every movement in your body, and it's like magic!

So, are you ready to join the Joyful Journeys of Mindful Movement? Get your dancing shoes on (or maybe just your comfy clothes!), and let's get moving!

. . .

Feel the joy in every stretch, embrace the rhythm of your breath, and dance like nobody's watching. It's time to explore the wonders of mindful movement and have a blast doing it!

Get ready to connect with your amazing body in the most fun and mindful way possible. Let the adventure begin, little movers and shakers! 🕺🦋🌟

5. DREAMY ADVENTURES: GUIDED VISUALIZATION FOR LITTLE EXPLORERS!

Hey there, little explorers! Are you ready for some exciting adventures in your imagination? It's time for "Guided Visualization" – a magical way to be mindful and let your creativity soar!

So, what's this cool activity all about? Well, it's like using the power of your imagination to go on fantastic journeys. Your parents or caregivers will take turns guiding you through serene and imaginative scenarios. How awesome is that?

Picture this: you close your eyes, and as they speak, you'll feel like you're right there in the story! You might go on a leisurely stroll through a lush forest, feeling the soft grass beneath your feet. Or maybe, you'll dive into an exciting underwater adventure surrounded by colorful sea creatures.

But wait, there's more! You can even float on a soft, fluffy cloud – like a daydream in the sky! It's like you're the hero of your very own story.

. . .

This journey is not just about listening – it's about using all your senses to make the adventure even more magical! You'll immerse yourself in the visualizations and feel like you're in a dream world.

And guess what? These dreamy adventures are like superhero training for your mind! They help you become more creative, think of amazing stories, and stay focused like a laser beam.

Guided Visualization is like a ticket to a world of endless possibilities. You'll learn to use your imagination to explore the wonders of your mind.

So, are you ready to join the Dreamy Adventures? Close your eyes, take a deep breath, and let the magic begin! Get ready to be mindful, creative, and go on the most incredible journeys ever!

It's time to discover the wonders of Guided Visualization, my little adventurers! Let's go on these dreamy trips together! 🌈🚀🦄

6. MAGICAL MINDFUL COLORING: WHERE ART AND MINDFULNESS UNITE!

Hey there, little artists! Have you heard about the enchanting world of mindful coloring? It's like a special journey where creativity meets mindfulness, and it's a whole lot of fun!

. . .

So, what's the deal with mindful coloring? Well, it's not just your typical coloring activity — it's a magical way to be totally present in the moment. Instead of rushing to finish a picture, you get to focus on the incredible process of coloring itself!

Imagine this: you hold your favorite coloring book and crayons in your hands. As you start to color, you'll notice something amazing — every little movement of your hand, every stroke of color, and every pattern that forms are all part of the adventure!

You might be wondering why this is special. Well, because it's all about being mindful — which means being super aware of the here and now. By paying close attention to the tiny details of coloring, you get to feel calm, focused, and relaxed.

And guess what? There's no right or wrong way to do it! You get to be your very own coloring master, creating beautiful art that's uniquely yours!

Mindful coloring is like a magic potion for your imagination and emotions. It helps you discover the joy in every color, the happiness in every stroke, and the wonder in the artistic world you create.

So, the next time you pick up your crayons and coloring book, remember to let your creativity flow like a sparkling river. Enjoy the journey of mindful coloring, and let your imagination take you to incredible places!

. . .

Let's embrace the world of mindful coloring together, where art and mindfulness unite in a marvelous adventure! Happy coloring, little artists!✋🖍️🧒

7. ADVENTURES IN EARTHING: DISCOVERING THE MAGIC BENEATH YOUR FEET!

Hey there, little adventurers! Let's embark on a thrilling journey called "Earthing" – it's like a magical connection with the Earth that can make you feel happier and healthier!

Imagine this: you take off your shoes and step onto the soft grass, warm sand, or squishy soil. Your bare feet touch the ground, and something wonderful happens – your body soaks up Earth's special energy! It's like getting a supercharged boost from nature herself!

But wait, what does this amazing adventure do for you? Well, it's not just a fun experience; it's filled with fantastic benefits too!

Physically, being barefoot on the Earth can help you sleep better, make your body feel less achy, and even make your immune system strong like a superhero shield!

And guess what? It's not just your body that feels the magic – your mind does too! Feeling connected with the Earth can make you feel calmer, less worried, and oh-so-happy! It's like having a picnic with your favorite friends, the trees and flowers.

. . .

Now, you might wonder how to go on this adventure. It's easy-peasy, lemon-squeezy! All you need to do is take off your shoes and find a cozy spot on the ground. It could be at the beach, in a park, or even in your very own backyard. The Earth is everywhere, ready to give you a big, warm hug!

Remember, being an Earthing adventurer is all about having fun and feeling good. So, don't forget to listen to your body, and you can even bring some friends along for the ride!

Are you ready to discover the magic beneath your feet? Let's go on this fantastic adventure together – the Earth is waiting to share its wonders with you! Happy Earthing, little nature explorers! 🌿🌍👣

HERE ARE MORE EXAMPLES:

Five Senses Exploration: Sit in a circle and take turns identifying five things you can see, hear, touch, smell, and taste around you.

Guided Imagery: Lead a visualization exercise, guiding participants to imagine peaceful and serene places.

Nature Walk: Go for a walk in nature, paying close attention to the sights, sounds, and smells around you.

Breath Counting: Practice counting breaths silently to bring focus and relaxation.

Bubble Breathing: Use bubble wands to blow bubbles slowly, focusing on each breath and watching the bubbles float away.

Body Scan: Lie down and bring awareness to each part of the body, releasing tension as you go.

Meditation Charades: Act out various mindfulness techniques while others guess what they are.

Mindful Eating: Enjoy a snack mindfully, savoring each bite and noticing the taste and texture.

Emotion Expression: Use drawing or writing to express emotions, then discuss them in a non-judgmental manner

Yoga for Kids: Incorporate simple yoga poses and movements that promote mindfulness and body awareness.

Peaceful Puppet Show: Create a puppet show that explores themes of kindness, empathy, and compassion.

Positive Affirmations: Have each person share positive affirmations about themselves and others.

Garden Meditation: Spend time tending to a garden, connecting with nature and the earth.

Cloud Watching: Lie on your back and observe the shapes of clouds, letting thoughts drift by like clouds in the sky.

Loving-Kindness Meditation: Practice sending love and well-wishes to oneself and others.

Gratitude Journal: Keep gratitude by jotting down things you are thankful for each day.

Meditation Storytelling: Tell stories with moral lessons that inspire mindfulness and reflection.

Remember, the goal is to make meditation enjoyable and accessible to everyone, so feel free to adapt these games to suit your group's preferences and needs.

. . .

While engaging children in these activities, it's essential to foster an environment of non-judgmental support, encouraging their free exploration of mindfulness. Open communication, active participation, and celebrating their efforts infuse a sense of achievement and fun into these games. It also gives them the confidence to continue exploring these mindfulness exercises.

Incorporating these games and exercises into your family routine transforms the process of learning meditation techniques into a memorable family journey. Not only do these activities instill valuable mindfulness skills in children, but they also serve as an adhesive, strengthening the bond among parents, caregivers, and children. The shared joy, combined with enhanced mindfulness, fosters a nurturing familial environment where everyone thrives emotionally, cognitively, and socially.

CHAPTER 11
MINDFUL BREATHING AND OTHER EXERCISES
JOURNEY INTO MINDFULNESS FOR CHILDREN

MINDFUL BREATHING EXERCISES serve as a simple yet powerful conduit to introduce children to the world of mindfulness. Among numerous techniques, the **"4-7-8 Breath"** is a fascinating method where participants breathe in for four counts, hold for seven, and exhale for eight counts. This exercise aids children in learning to regulate their breathing, aiding them in cultivating calmness and focus.

EMBARKING ON A BREATHING ADVENTURE: THE 4-7-8 BREATH EXERCISE

The 4-7-8 Breath technique is akin to a magical spell of tranquility, leading children on an adventure to inner peace and focus. This exercise unfolds like an engaging narrative, enabling children to connect with their breath in a playful yet meaningful way.

Begin by inviting children to find a cozy position that allows them to be relaxed yet alert. Encourage them to tune into their breath, taking deep and calming inhalations. This initial stage prepares them for their imminent journey into mindful breathing.

The first step in this magical adventure involves a deep inhalation for a count of four. As they breathe in, children are encouraged to feel their lungs expand, much like a balloon. This inhalation fills their bodies with a sense of wonder and curiosity, setting the stage for the next phase.

Next, guide the children to hold their breath for a count of seven. In this silent pause, they're encouraged to envision themselves floating amidst tranquil clouds, embodying serenity and lightness. This pause allows them to connect with the peaceful silence that resides within, promoting an appreciation for stillness.

Finally, it's time for them to release their breath, gently exhaling to the count of eight. This breath release is associated with letting go of any stress, worries, or tension, paving the way for a sense of calm and ease. Children can imagine a gentle breeze carrying away their concerns, making space for peace and tranquility.

Throughout this exercise, encourage children to utilize their vivid imaginations. Let them visualize themselves as graceful trees swaying with each breath, becoming still like majestic mountains as they pause and release their breath like magical bubbles carrying away their worries.

. . .

Help children to notice the subtle sensations that arise with their focused breathing. Whether it's the rise and fall of their bellies or the gentle rush of air through their noses, invite them to become observers of their own breath, fostering a sense of calm and relaxation.

Once the exercise concludes, gently guide them back to their surroundings, inviting them to notice the residual calmness within, a delightful souvenir from their breathing adventure.

Remember to bring an element of playfulness into these exercises, using imaginative language and imagery to make the process captivating for children. By engaging in such mindful breathing exercises, children can learn to appreciate the magic of their breath, harnessing its power to bring tranquility and focus into their lives.

INTERACTIVE MINDFULNESS GAMES AND ACTIVITIES

Incorporating mindfulness games and activities into children's daily routines can enhance their engagement with meditation and mindfulness. Games like **"Mindful Listening,"** where children are encouraged to identify the variety of sounds around them, promote focus and awareness, enhancing their attention skills.

Another exciting game is **"Mindful Eating,"** encouraging children to eat slowly while paying attention to the flavors, textures, and sensations experienced during their meals. This practice can foster a more mindful approach to eating, promoting healthier eating habits and a positive relationship with food.

· · ·

Guided meditations like **"The Magic Carpet Ride"** or "The Enchanted Forest" provide an imaginary journey that fosters relaxation, visualization, and mindfulness. These guided meditations, tailored for children, offer an engaging way to introduce them to the world of mindfulness.

By including these games and exercises in their routines, parents and caregivers can aid their children in developing foundational meditation and mindfulness skills. Not only do these activities serve as a fun, family bonding experiences, but they also nurture a positive relationship with children's thoughts and emotions. Such techniques can have lasting effects on children's mental health and well-being, fostering their growth and development in a mindful, balanced way.

CHAPTER 12
GUIDED MEDITATION EXERCISES
RAINBOW MEDITATION: A GUIDED MEDITATION EXERCISE FOR CHILDREN

GUIDED meditation exercises are powerful tools to introduce children to meditation, harnessing their vivid imaginations to encourage focus, calm, and emotional regulation. A fantastic example of such an exercise is the "Rainbow Meditation," a vibrant, immersive journey through colors that promotes a sense of balance and harmony in both body and mind.

EMBARKING ON THE JOURNEY: RAINBOW MEDITATION

The Rainbow Meditation unfolds like a captivating storybook, inviting children on an exciting adventure through a radiant landscape of colors. As they journey through the spectrum, children learn to associate different colors with various feelings and states of being, simultaneously enhancing their visualization skills.

To begin, invite the children to find a peaceful spot where they can sit or lie down comfortably. Encourage them to gently close their eyes, letting go of the external world as they prepare to embark on their colorful adventure.

INHALING COLORS: THE RAINBOW JOURNEY

Now, begin to weave the tale of the grand rainbow stretching across the sky, with each color blending into the next, forming a dazzling spectacle. Vividly describe each shade, starting with the robust reds, moving through the oranges, yellows, greens, blues, indigos, and finally reaching the profound violets.

As children take in your descriptions, invite them to imagine breathing in each color, associating every hue with unique qualities.

Red: Energy and Strength

As they breathe in the vibrant red color, children visualize a warming glow imbuing their bodies with energy and strength. This visual imagery cultivates a sense of vitality, invigorating their minds and bodies.

Orange: Joy and Creativity

Next, children are guided to inhale the lively orange, envisaging a dynamic light that fuels their creativity and instills a sense of joy, stimulating their imaginative abilities and encouraging a positive mindset.

Yellow: Warmth and Optimism

When children breathe in the sunny yellow, they're asked to

imagine a brilliant light radiating warmth and optimism. This visual exercise creates a sense of positivity and cheer, brightening their outlook.

Green: Balance and Tranquility

Moving on to the calming green, children envision a serene wave of tranquility washing over them, fostering balance and peace, grounding their energy, and encouraging a calm state of mind.

Blue: Clarity and Peace

As they inhale the soothing blue, children visualize a refreshing breeze gently wafting over them. The blue light represents clarity and peace, cleansing their thoughts and promoting serene introspection.

Indigo: Intuition and Wisdom

Breathing in the profound indigo, children are guided to envisage an enchanting glow sparking their intuition and wisdom. The indigo light encourages them to trust their instincts and bolsters their confidence in their inner voice.

Violet: Spirituality and Connection

Finally, as they breathe in the majestic violet, children imagine a radiant light enveloping them, symbolizing spirituality and connectivity. This visualization fosters a sense of awe and deepens their connection to the world, cultivating a sense of unity and oneness.

CONCLUSION OF THE JOURNEY

To conclude the meditation, guide children to slowly open their eyes, gently returning to their surroundings. Encourage them to share their colorful experiences, fostering a sense of connection and camaraderie. This reflection allows children to express their feelings and experiences, promoting open communication and shared understanding.

Remember, the key to an effective Rainbow Meditation is to use playful language and evocative descriptions, sparking children's imaginations. By engaging with the colors and their associated emotions and qualities, children can explore their inner world, develop impressive visualization skills, and learn to regulate their emotions. The enchanting journey of Rainbow Meditation thus serves as a bridge, connecting children to the powerful world of meditation and mindfulness.

PART 4: PRACTICAL APPLICATIONS

Cultivating Mindfulness in Children Through Daily Practices
　"The Colourful Journey: Mindful Colouring Adventures"
　"The Whimsical Adventure of Muscle Relaxation"
　"The Adventure of Sir Mindful: A Tale of Meditation and Mindfulness"
　Making Mindfulness a Joyful Family Journey
　Games for Children to Learn Meditation
　Meditation Magic: A Family's Path to Peace and Happiness

CHAPTER 13
CULTIVATING MINDFULNESS IN CHILDREN THROUGH DAILY PRACTICES

IN TODAY'S FAST-PACED WORLD, children face increasing distractions that can disrupt their focus, heighten anxiety, and stir restlessness. The ability to tune into the present moment mindfully has become an invaluable skill for children to cultivate.

> According to mindfulness experts, "Mindfulness practice helps children improve attention, calm anxiety, handle stress, regulate emotions, be kind, and make good choices" (Williams et al., 2012).

For children, mindfulness is best nurtured through brief, engaging practices woven seamlessly into their daily routines. In this chapter, we provide parents and caregivers with practical guidance on incorporating mindfulness into the fabric of children's lives. We share techniques tailored for different age groups that develop self-regulation, sensory awareness, sustained focus, and compassion. Our aim is to empower you with strategies to help your children reap the amazing benefits of mindfulness as a way of life.

WHY DAILY MINDFULNESS MATTERS

> "Mindfulness is like learning to play the piano. The more you practice, the better you get at being mindful and the more it enhances your life," (Sweet & Miles, 2021)

She notes that mindfulness changes the structure and functioning of the brain to support well-being.

> Indeed, studies using MRI scans have detected increased density and activity in brain regions linked to learning, memory, executive function, and emotional processing in regular meditators (Medicine et al., 2020)

Daily mindfulness practices stimulate these cognitive, emotional, and interpersonal skills in developing brains.

Additionally, mindfulness strengthens neural connections between the limbic system, the emotional center, and the prefrontal cortex, which governs executive function.

"This boosts children's capacity to observe feelings compassionately and respond thoughtfully rather than reacting impulsively" (Allen et al., 2021)

Beyond neurological changes, research shows that consistent mindfulness practice decreases stress and anxiety, while improving concentration, self-esteem, sleep quality, and social skills in children and adolescents (Fancourt & Finn, 2019).

Integrating simple practices into daily routines maximizes these benefits.

By making mindfulness part of children's habits early on, parents provide the gift of emotional tools that will serve them for a lifetime. Just as daily exercise builds children's physical health, regular mindfulness strengthens their mental and emotional fitness.

MORNING MINDFULNESS PRACTICES

The morning offers a perfect opportunity to start the day with mindfulness as it sets the stage for children's mood and behavior. Some easy practices to try:

Mindful awakening

- Instead of jumping out of bed, guide children to take a few deep breaths, stretch slowly, and tune into the sensations in their bodies as they wake up. This allows for a gradual and tranquil transition into the day.

Gratitude sharing

- At breakfast, take turns sharing one thing you feel grateful for today—whether it's a friend, a favorite toy, something in nature, or even a simple comfort like a warm bath. This cultivates appreciation and positivity.

Five senses check-in

- As children eat breakfast, prompt them to notice five things they can see, hear, touch, smell, and taste in that moment. Heightening sensory awareness brings their attention to the present.

Walking meditation

- While walking to school or the bus stop, encourage mindful steps, focusing on the sensations in their feet and legs as they slowly move forward. Feelings of calm and body awareness can carry through the commute.

Affirmation practice

- Before parting for the day, take a minute to exchange words of encouragement and affirmation such as, "You've got this!" or "You shine so bright!" This instills confidence to take on the day.

BEDTIME MINDFULNESS PRACTICES

The bedtime routine offers a window to wind down, release stress, and transition peacefully into sleep. Weave in these practices:

Body scan
- Lying in bed, guide children to slowly scan their body from toes to head, noticing any areas of tightness and allowing their body to relax and unwind. This fosters physical calmness and body awareness.

Mindful reading
- Include children's books about mindfulness as part of quiet reading time before bed. Listening attentively to stories promotes stillness and reflection.

Loving-kindness
- Try ending the day wishing loved ones sweet dreams and sending silent blessings such as "May you be happy" or "May you feel peace." These positive intentions infuse a sense of warmth, gratitude, and connection.

Gratitude journaling
- Take a few minutes to jot down or discuss positive moments or things learned throughout the day. Reflecting on the joys and gifts of the day cultivates gratitude and optimism.

. . .

Calm breathing
- Practice square breathing together— inhaling for 4 counts, holding for 4 counts, exhaling for 4 counts, and pausing for 4 counts. This simple, rhythmic breath exercise induces relaxation and restful sleep.

MEALTIME MINDFULNESS

Drawing awareness to the senses during meals offers children invaluable lessons in savoring the moment, appreciating food, and training focus. Try these techniques:

Mindful tasting
- One bite at a time, guide children to slowly taste their food, exploring flavors and textures by chewing extra slowly. This presence heightens their eating experience and satisfaction.

Gratitude ritual
- Before eating, hold hands and take a moment to express gratitude—whether for the food itself, the people who prepared it, or even the farmers who grew it. Appreciating the web of life that sustains us builds humility.

Calm eating
- Encourage children to pause and take at least one to three deep breaths before each bite, then to chew thoroughly before swallowing. This prevents overeating and promotes digestion.

. . .

Pleasant conversation
- Meals offer the perfect time for lighthearted family chats. Avoid scolding or criticism during this time, which can condition kids to associate eating with stress. Keep it positive!

Five senses
Ask children to notice 5 things they can see, hear, smell, touch, and taste during the meal. Sharpening sensory awareness enhances their enjoyment and bonds them to the present.

Mindfulness on the Go!
Weave mindfulness into little pockets of time throughout the day:

Short breath awareness
- Set a chime timer to ring a few times during the day as a reminder to pause and take 5 conscious breaths. These micro-practices build mindfulness habits.

Nature moments
- When outside, encourage children to pause and observe the plants, trees, animals, and sky around them. Communing with nature is meditative.

Mindful transitions
- The bus, in between activities or while in line, are opportuni-

ties to tune into the body or breath for a minute. These small gaps can be mindfulness openings.

Gratitude sharing

- Before dinner or at bedtime, have each person take turns sharing something that made them feel grateful that day. Cultivates empathy and positivity.

One-minute body scan

- While in the car, waiting in line, or during transitions, guide children to quickly scan their body and release any tension.

Mindful listening

- When readings stories at bedtime, occasionally pause and ask children to listen closely for subtle sounds in the environment. Develops concentration.

Heartfulness

- Briefly place a hand over the heart and guide children to silently send good wishes to someone in need. Grows compassion.

Daily mindfulness practices can be integrated seamlessly once they become a habit. The amount of time matters less than the consistency. Even starting with 1-2 minutes a day stimulates brain benefits!

TAILORING MINDFULNESS FOR DIFFERENT AGES

Children's capacities and needs vary across developmental stages. Understanding general capabilities at each age allows for practices to be tailored appropriately.

Toddlers (1-3 years):

- Short duration (30 seconds to 2 minutes)
    - Simple breathing exercises using visuals and play
    - Movement-based: dancing, stretching
    - Nature interaction: touching leaves, flowers
    - Verbal guidance and mirroring by caregivers

Preschoolers (3-5 years):

- Duration of 2-5 minutes
    - Engaging visuals and props like stuffed animal breaths
    - Interactive games like mindful counting
    - Imaginative journeys to engage creatively
    - Child-led movement: yoga, walking meditation
    - Verbal cues and guidance from caregivers

Early grade school (6-9 years):

. . .

- Duration of 5-10 minutes
    - Calming breathing routines: balloon or wave visualization
    - Body awareness activities: progressive muscle relaxation
    - Creativity based: mindful drawing, origami
    - Introduce sitting, walking meditation
    - Discuss concepts simply - impermanence, gratitude

Pre-teens (10-12 years):

- Duration of 10-15 minutes
    - Breath-focused meditation
    - Body scans and yoga for adolescents
    - Expand concepts: interconnection, compassion
    - Increase silent periods, decrease guidance
    - Cultivate a consistent home practice
    - Make space for reflection and discussion

Teens (13-18 years):

- 15-20 minute seated meditation
    - Mindful movement: qi gong, tai chi
    - Discuss philosophy: mindfulness insights
    - Mindful technology use
    - Manage challenging emotions and self-talk
    - Set personal intentions and goals
    - Respect the desire for autonomy in practice

- Provide guidance as needed

While these age frameworks offer direction, always allow your child's temperament, needs, and evolving capacity to guide the mindfulness techniques you introduce.

CREATING A MINDFUL SPACE

To fully reap the benefits, children need to practice mindfulness in an environment that feels safe, calm, and comforting. Some key elements include:

Minimal distractions

- Turn off screens, phones, and loud music to cultivate quiet. Ambient nature sounds can support settling in.

Comfortable space

- Allow a flexible posture - sitting, lying down, or even walking. Avoid rigidity. Prioritize comfort to let the body relax.

Soothing aesthetic

- Incorporate soft lighting, blankets, pillows, and nature elements like plants or flowers to create coziness.

Supportive guidance

- Offer occasional verbal cues if needed, but allow most practices to unfold in silence. Avoid criticism of their efforts.

. . .

Positive reinforcement
 - Provide specific praise when children demonstrate mindful behaviors to motivate consistency: "I noticed you took some deep breaths when you got angry. Nice job!"

Family participation
 - Having the whole family engage together generates enthusiasm. Children often learn mindfulness best by observation.

Consistency
 - A regular time and quiet space signals the transition into mindfulness. This consistency and ritual primes the mind-body for relaxation.

Through developing a nurturing physical and emotional environment, mindfulness practice becomes a moment children eagerly anticipate rather than dread. Setting them up for success ensures meaningful engagement and continuity.

TROUBLESHOOTING CHALLENGES

Introducing mindfulness to children inevitably brings some bumps along the road. Some typical challenges and how to address them:

The child seems bored or restless
 - Keep practices brief and engaging. Add tactile elements the

child can hold or manipulate, such as breathing Buddies. Offer choices between methods.

Too much energy
- Incorporate gentle movements like mindful walking or stretching. Practice after physical play when energy levels are lower. Guide children in noticing and naming their restlessness.

Short attention span
- Try shorter 1-2 minute segments with structure and repetition. Use captivating visualizations related to their interests. Notice and praise when their focus returns after wandering.

Self-consciousness
- Normalize distraction and patience with oneself. Emphasize that mindfulness is just noticing thoughts and feelings without judgment. Keep practices enjoyable to reduce performance anxiety.

Resistance
- Move at the child's pace. Never force participation. Keep it light-hearted. Focus on modeling mindfulness yourself. Their resistance will often naturally subside if given time.

Difficulty naming feelings
- Provide examples of how emotions manifest physically, such as anger causing clenched fists. Use creative outlets like drawing to

aid emotional identification. Offer validation for all expressed feelings.

Impatience with slow progress
   - Remember, mindfulness is a skill developed over the years. Trust the process. Small steps still confer benefits. Meet them where they are with compassion.

By addressing concerns with empathy and creativity vs. punishment, children come to see mindfulness as supporting rather than controlling them. Have faith in their inner wisdom to embrace the practices that resonate at their own tempo.

THE HEART OF THE MATTER: LOVING-KINDNESS PRACTICE

While various techniques help children enhance their focus, calm, and awareness, mindfulness also offers practices specifically designed to cultivate kindness and compassion. Known as metta or loving-kindness meditation, these practices involve sending goodwill and warm wishes toward oneself and others.

According to researcher Dr. Richie Davidson of the University of Wisconsin, Madison, "Research shows that practicing loving-kindness meditation increases love, joy, contentment, gratitude, pride, hope, interest, amusement and awe" (The Science of Mindfulness, 2022). It builds bonds with others and amplifies positive emotions.

Loving-kindness practices use the repetition of mantras or phrases as an anchor to reinforce feelings of benevolence. Two simple examples appropriate for children:

Self-compassion

> "May I be happy.
> May I be peaceful.
> May I be safe.
> May I be free."

Universal compassion

> "May all beings be happy. May all beings be peaceful. May all beings be safe. May all beings be free."

These mantras can be recited silently or aloud while envisioning the recipient surrounded in light and warmth.

> Combining words with visualization strengthens neural patterns that support empathy, which is beneficial for emotional and social intelligence (Ford & Smith, 2020).

Even simpler phrases work well too. Have children silently wish others,

"I hope you're happy."

or

"I hope you feel better soon."

Wishes can be sent to loved ones, classmates, neighbors, crying babies, or animals in need of comfort.

Support children in identifying times when they wish they had received compassion. Then prompt them to become the giver, sending themselves the kindness they seek. By cultivating loving-kindness, children evolve from simply wishing others would understand to embodying the understanding themselves.

Through committed daily practice, loving-kindness seeps into children's subconscious, subtly influencing how they relate to themselves and others. It provides an inner compass orienting them toward wisdom, empathy, and grace.

CONCLUSION

In closing, integrating mindfulness into the fabric of children's daily lives profoundly nourishes their development and well-being. Yet it is not a chore to squeeze in, but a way of being. By gently guiding children to pause and reconnect with their breathing, body, feelings, and senses throughout the day, parents help reshape their relationship with themselves and the world in a more positive light.

Mindfulness provides children with an inner refuge to return to amidst the rush and complexities of daily life. As parents, when we model mindfulness ourselves, we demonstrate that stillness and serenity are always accessible within. By planting these seeds of peace as family daily practices, we enable our children to increasingly draw upon this inner wisdom as their foundation, guiding them to live with greater heartfulness, focus, and joy.

"THE COLOURFUL JOURNEY: MINDFUL COLOURING ADVENTURES"
STORY

"The Colourful Journey: Mindful Colouring Adventures"

© 2023 Foss Plus. All rights reserved.

Mindful Colouring Exercises

It was a bright and sunny Saturday morning when best friends Ava, Noah, and Sophie gathered at Ava's house for their weekly art session. Ava's mom had set up a big table in the living room covered in coloring books, markers, crayons, and printed coloring sheets.

> "Wow, look at all this!"

Exclaimed Noah.

> "There's so much to choose from!"

The three friends took a moment to browse through the pile of coloring books, oohing and aahing over the variety of images. Sophie picked up a book filled with intricate mandala designs.

> "These are so cool. I can't wait to make them burst with color!"

Noah grabbed a book with images of race cars and planes.

> "Check out these awesome vehicles! I'm going to make them look so realistic."

Ava smiled as she flipped through a fairy tale coloring book.

> "I love these fantasy scenes. It'll be like stepping into a magical world."

After gathering their supplies, the three friends found comfortable spots around the table. Ava sat up nice and tall, imagining herself as a regal fairy queen. Noah sprawled out on the floor, surrounded by pillows, picturing himself flying planes and racing cars. Sophie curled up in a cozy armchair, ready to let her creativity unfold.

Before beginning, they closed their eyes and took a deep breath to focus their minds. As they slowly exhaled, they let go of any worries or distractions, fully immersing themselves in the present moment.

> "Alright, are you ready for a mindful coloring adventure?"

Asked Ava.

"You bet!"

Said Noah.

"I'm ready to bring these vehicles to life!"

"Let's make some magic,"

Sophie added with a smile.

The three got to work, carefully choosing their colors and slowly bringing the black-and-white images to life. With each stroke of their markers, they focused their attention completely on the sensation of the tip gliding across the paper. The sweet fruity smell of the markers filled the air as they steadily colored and shaded the intricate designs.

Occasionally, their minds would drift off, distracted by daydreams or wandering thoughts. But just like expert jugglers, they gently guided their focus back to the present moment and the coloring page in front of them.

"Oops, I got a little carried away thinking about ice cream."

Laughed Sophie.

"Back to the mandalas!"

"I know, it's so easy for my mind to wander."

Said Ava. "Let's get centered again."
Noah added,

> "It's kind of like playing hide and seek with our thoughts. Gotta catch them and bring them back to the coloring!"

The minutes slipped by as the three friends colored in peaceful silence, interrupted only by the scratching of markers on paper. Sunbeams streamed in through the windows, bathing everything in a warm glow.

After some time, they began to put the final touches on their artwork. Sophie added some metallic gel pens to make her mandalas sparkle. Noah grabbed some colored pencils to add texture and dimension to his vehicles. Ava switched to oil pastels to shade the wings of the fairies in her coloring book.

> "Check it out, my cars are ready to race off the page!"

Said Noah.

> "Ooh your fairies look so magical."

Added Sophie.

> "I can practically see their wings fluttering."

> "And your mandalas are hypnotizing me with their patterns."

Said Ava.

> "Great job, everyone!"

The three friends held up their finished coloring pages, admiring each other's creative talents. As they reflected on their mindful coloring session, they realized how calm, focused, and happy they felt. The act of coloring deliberately while staying rooted in the present moment filled them with a sense of peaceful joy.

> "That was so relaxing, I could color for hours,"

Noah said while stretching his arms overhead.

> "Me too; I feel so centered and tranquil."

Said Sophie.
Ava nodded in agreement.

> "It's amazing how coloring mindfully can make you feel. I learned that it helps me focus on the present instead of worrying about other things."

> "It unlocks my creativity, too."

Added Noah.

> "I get so immersed in bringing the images to life with color."

> "It's like a form of meditation."

Mused Sophie.

> "A relaxing journey into imagination and creativity."

The three friends decided to make mindful coloring sessions a regular part of their weekly art gatherings. They realized that by practicing mindfulness - paying attention to their thoughts and sensations in the present moment - while coloring, they could cultivate feelings of inner calmness and contentment. It was a perfect way to tap into their creative spirits while cultivating gratitude.

> "Same time next week?"

Asked Ava.

> "YOU BET!"

Said Noah and Sophie in unison.

As they began cleaning up their coloring station, the three friends felt a newfound sense of closeness. They deepened their bond while nurturing their minds and creativity through the simple act of mindful coloring. And they now had a go-to activity for those times when they needed to refocus, relax, and reconnect with the present moment.

So the next time you feel like you need to hit the reset button, consider embarking on your own mindful coloring adventure. Let your imagination run free as you focus your attention on the sensations of your coloring tools gliding across the page. Discover inner peace as you bring black and white images to life with vibrant color. Mindfulness and creativity go hand in hand. Just as Noah, Sophie, and Ava learned, mindful coloring can guide you to a world of tranquility, gratitude, and childlike joy.

The End

"THE WHIMSICAL ADVENTURE OF MUSCLE RELAXATION"
STORY

© 2023 Foss Plus. All rights reserved.

"The Whimsical Adventure of Muscle Relaxation"

It was a lazy Sunday afternoon, and best friends Zoe, Leah, and Ben were hanging out at Zoe's house. After a busy week of school, sports, and activities, the three 12-year-olds were ready for some rest and relaxation.

"I'm so stressed out and tense from this past week,"

complained Leah, rubbing her sore shoulders.

"I wish I could just shake all this tension away."

"Me too; I feel like I have knots all over from soccer practice,"

said, Ben.

"We need to do something to relax."

Zoe's face lit up with an idea.

"Guys, why don't we go on a whimsical adventure of muscle relaxation? I read about this super fun mindfulness activity that helps you release physical tension from head to toe."

"A muscle relaxation adventure? I like the sound of that!"

said, Leah.
Ben nodded in agreement.

"I'm down for anything if it helps me feel less stressed."

The three-headed up to Zoe's room to begin their relaxing quest. They changed into comfy clothes and grabbed some blankets and pillows to make the atmosphere extra cozy.

"First, we need to find a super chill relax-mode spot"

Instructed Zoe as they arranged pillows and blankets on the floor.

Once their nest was complete, the friends lay down on their backs and closed their eyes. Zoe led them through a deep breathing exercise to begin centering their minds for the relaxation journey.

> "Okay, imagine you're a sloth preparing for a long, blissful nap in the jungle,"

said Zoe in a soft, soothing voice.

> "Breathe in slowly through your nose and feel your lungs fill up with air like balloons."

Leah, Ben, and Zoe all took in long, slow inhales, envisioning their lungs inflating.

> "Now gently breathe out through your mouth, deflating the balloons,"

continued Zoe.

> "Feel your body start to sink into the floor, completely relaxed."

They exhaled calmly, feeling their muscles begin to loosen.

> "Now we're ready for the muscle relaxation adventure to begin,"

said, Zoe.

> "I'll guide you through tensing and relaxing each body part."

> "Let's do it!"

Said Leah eagerly.

> "Count me in,"

added Ben.

> "This already feels soothing."

> "First up...toes!"

announced Zoe.

> "Imagine your toes are playing hide-and-seek. On the count of three, squeeze and curl them in tight to hide from the seeker. One...two...three, curl your toes!"

Ben, Leah, and Zoe all scrunched their toes tightly, feeling the tension build.

> "Great job hiding those toes!"

praised Zoe.

> "Now release them and relax completely. Let all the tightness melt away."

The three friends uncurled their toes, letting the tension go. They felt a calming sense of relief wash over their feet.

> "Ahhh, my toes feel so relaxed,"

sighed Leah blissfully.

> "Mine too; that was an awesome first round,"

said, Ben.

"Alright, now picture your feet as superheroes trying to protect a precious treasure,"

instructed Zoe.

"When I say go, curl them in tight to keep the treasure safe. Three...two...one...go, curl!"

They flexed their feet inward, squeezing hard.

"Okay, superhero feet, you can relax! Release the tension,"

said Zoe after a few seconds.

Their feet went limp as they released the squeeze.

Zoe continued guiding them through tensing and relaxing each body part, using playful imagery to keep them engaged. They squeezed their legs together like koalas hugging a tree. They tightened their stomachs like they were wearing superhero abs. They hugged their arms like penguins trying to stay warm.

Each time, the tension melted away as they relaxed again, leaving them feeling increasingly loose and relieved. After relaxing their fingers, arms, shoulders, and facial muscles, they took a few minutes to rest in total body tranquility.

"Wow, I feel like I'm floating on a cloud right now,"

murmured Ben dreamily.

"That was amazing."

"Seriously, I don't think I've ever been this relaxed before in my life," said, Leah.

> "My mind feels so calm too."

> "We definitely need to make this muscle relaxation adventure a regular thing,"

suggested Zoe.
Her two friends nodded their heads in eager agreement.

Over the next few weeks, the three friends set aside time to embark on their imagination-fueled relaxation journeys. No matter how chaotic their days had been, they found that the muscle relaxation activity brought them back to a state of harmony and ease.

They looked forward to their cozy relaxation sessions, where they could escape stress and tension through the simple act of tensing and releasing their muscles. It became a treasured time to bond as friends while also caring for their mental and physical well-being.

One evening, during a sleepover at Leah's house, they decided to take their relaxation ritual up a notch. After dimming the lights, they grabbed eye masks and ambient nature sounds to enhance the experience.

> "I feel like I'm one with nature right now,"

whispered Ben as soft forest sounds filled the room.

> "Shhh, no talking, just relax,"

Leah gently admonished.
They tensed and relaxed their way from head to toe, melting

deeper into tranquility with each body part. The eye masks helped minimize visual distractions, allowing them to focus inward.

By the end, they felt almost hypnotized by the total mind and body serenity. As the last bit of tension left their bodies, they drifted off to sleep, happily nestled together.

The three friends learned an invaluable skill through their whimsical muscle relaxation adventures. They discovered the magic of being able to ease both physical and mental stress through simple breathing and muscle exercises.

While life got busy and chaotic at times, they knew they always had a relaxation ritual to come back to. Their imagination-powered, tension-taming journeys became a source of comradery, creativity, and calm.

So the next time you're feeling stressed and tense, why not set off on your own whimsical relaxation quest? Let your imagination be the guide as you dissolve tension from head to toe. Discover the relaxing superpowers that have been within your body all along. Your mind and muscles will thank you!

The END

"THE ADVENTURE OF SIR MINDFUL: A TALE OF MEDITATION AND MINDFULNESS"
STORY

© 2023 Foss Plus. All rights reserved.

The Legend of Sir Mindful and the Mindfulness Dragon

In a small village nestled in a tranquil valley, there lived a young boy named Finn who dreamed of becoming a brave and noble knight. He idolized the tales of chivalrous knights vanquishing dragons and saving damsels in distress. If only he could be as courageous as the heroes in those stories, Finn thought.

One morning, Finn was tending to the sheep in the meadow when he noticed a peculiar sight - a figure dressed in shining armor approaching on horseback. As the knight drew nearer, Finn saw that his armor was not metal, but rather shimmered like dragon scales. Upon his chest was emblazoned a crest in the shape of a lotus flower.

> "Greetings, young one,"

Spoke the knight in a warm, friendly voice.

> "My name is Sir Mindful, and I am on a quest to spread the teachings of mindfulness throughout the land."

Finn could hardly contain his excitement.

> "Wow, Sir Mindful, it's an honor to meet you! I want to become a brave knight too. Will you teach me your ways?"

Sir Mindful chuckled.

> "Of course, my friend. Mindfulness is a skill that takes time and practice to cultivate. Let us begin our first lesson here and now - mindful breathing."

The pair sat together on the soft grass. Following Sir Mindful's guidance, Finn focused on his breath, noticing the gentle rise and fall of his chest. When his mind wandered, he gently escorted it back to the present. Finn felt his body relax into a state of tranquility.

After some time, Sir Mindful spoke again,

> "Excellent work, Finn. The key is to anchor yourself in the here and now, not get tangled in worries of the past or future. This mindful presence will serve you well on your journey."

At that moment, Finn knew that this was the mentor he had been waiting for.

Over the next few weeks, Finn met with Sir Mindful daily to continue his mindfulness training. They practiced mindful movement, walking slowly and intentionally through the forest. They did mindful listening exercises, tuning into the symphony of nature. With each lesson, Finn grew more focused, patient, and in touch with his surroundings.

Then one day, their peace was shattered by the bloodcurdling roar of a dragon overhead. The massive beast circled the meadow, spewing fireballs. Finn trembled, but Sir Mindful rested a hand on his shoulder.

> "Be still, Finn. This dragon is not our enemy; rather, she is misunderstood. We must approach her with mindfulness and empathy."

Sir Mindful walked calmly into the meadow, unaffected by the dragon's intimidating display. He simply sat cross-legged on the grass and closed his eyes, grounding himself in meditative stillness. Intrigued, the dragon settled onto the ground near the tranquil knight.

> "Dragon, we mean you no harm."

Sir Mindful said.

> "Something must be causing you pain. Will you share your story so we may understand?"

The dragon peered curiously at Sir Mindful. In all her centuries of life, no one had ever tried to communicate with her before. She sensed the knight's compassion.

In a gravelly voice, the dragon explained that humans had attacked and destroyed her home many years ago. Since then, anger and bitterness have dwelled within her. Sir Mindful listened intently, seeing the suffering beneath the dragon's ferocity.

> "You have endured much hardship."

Replied Sir Mindful.

> "But as we practice mindfulness, we learn that holding onto resentment only breeds more pain. May we sit together in meditation? Perhaps we can find a new way forward."

Moved by his kind words, the dragon agreed. Finn watched in awe as the knight and dragon sat together, eyes closed in tranquil meditation. Their shared mindfulness calmed the rage and sadness that gripped the dragon's heart. For the first time in ages, she felt a flicker of hope.

From that day on, the dragon became an ally to Sir Mindful and Finn. With her help, they traveled the land spreading the message of mindfulness and compassion. The dragon taught them to see situations from new perspectives. And when faced with conflict, they approached adversaries with empathy rather than aggression.

Finn blossomed under their guidance, his inner courage and conviction strengthening each day. He took Sir Mindful's lessons to heart, dealing with life's challenges by grounding himself in the present moment.

One day, Finn knew that he was ready to embark on his own crusade as a mindfulness knight. Before leaving, he turned to Sir Mindful.

> "I owe all I have become to your teachings. You showed me that true bravery comes from within. A mindful heart and open mind can overcome any foe."

Sir Mindful placed a hand on Finn's shoulder.

> "You learned well, brave knight. Now go and spread this message of peace far and wide."

The dragon approached and bowed her head in reverence to Finn, appointing him as her noble rider. As Finn rode off on the dragon's back, Sir Mindful and his apprentice exchanged one final smile. They knew that the future shone brightly for this young knight and all those whose lives he would touch.

Finn and the dragon traveled through misty valleys, sun-kissed meadows, and mossy forests, stopping to meditate with all who wished to learn the transformative power of mindfulness. Through their courage and compassion, they turned former foes into faithful friends.

Years passed, and tales spread far and wide of the brave young Knight Finn and his mythical dragon spreading their light wherever they went. Their legend reminds us that when faced with life's challenges, we need only pause, take a mindful breath, and meet the situation with wisdom and empathy. For within each of us lies the capacity to transform ourselves and our world for the better.

The End.

CHAPTER 14
MAKING MINDFULNESS A JOYFUL FAMILY JOURNEY
MAKING MINDFULNESS A JOYFUL FAMILY JOURNEY

INTRODUCING children to the world of mindfulness is an exciting journey - one filled with discovery, bonding, and fun! In this chapter, we'll explore creative ways for parents and caregivers to engage children in simple, playful mindfulness practices. You'll find a toolbox of engaging activities suitable for kids of all ages.

We'll also dive into practical guidance on overcoming common obstacles, setting kids up for success, and weaving mindfulness into family life. Our aim is to empower you to make mindfulness an enjoyable shared experience that brings your family closer together!

WHY MAKE IT A FAMILY AFFAIR?

Practicing mindfulness together generates benefits on many levels. Studies show that when parents model mindfulness, children are more likely to embrace the practices, too (Parent et al., 2016).

Beyond leading by example, sharing these experiences as a family helps make mindfulness seem more accessible to kids. They see practice as just a part of everyday life rather than a chore.

Family participation also enhances bonding. Simple practices like gratitude sharing at dinnertime lead to heartwarming moments that strengthen connections. Laughter during mindful games fosters joyful memories. And guided meditations before bedtime can become cherished rituals.

In addition, non-competitive mindfulness activities provide a screen-free way to engage children that focuses on their inner world. Forging these strong relationships in the present will serve families for years to come.

TAILORING MINDFULNESS: AGES AND STAGES

To create a meaningful experience for every member, it helps to consider appropriate techniques based on age and ability. Here is a general guide:

Ages 2-4: Short, playful activities (1-5 minutes); simple stretching or breathing; verbal guidance; sensory nature interaction.

. . .

Ages 5-7: Interactive games, imagination journeys (5-10 minutes); introduce mindful movement; discuss simple concepts like gratitude.

Ages 8-10: Longer practices (10-15 minutes); breath-focused exercises; loving-kindness practices; encourage journaling.

Ages 11-14: Seated meditation; mindful technology use; loving-kindness for challenging emotions; respect growing autonomy.

Keep in mind that these are flexible frameworks. Allow your child's needs and evolving capacities to guide you. Move at their developmental pace.

SETTING THE STAGE FOR SUCCESS

For kids to fully engage, some simple adjustments can make all the difference:

- **Offer choices:** Let children select the type of practice they would enjoy. Shared control builds enthusiasm.

- **Prioritize comfort:** Allow flexible postures - sitting, lying down, or walking. Avoid rigidity.

. . .

- **Minimize distractions:** Turn off screens and loud sounds. Ambient nature audio can help calm the space.

- **Add cozy elements:** Incorporate blankets, soothing lighting, plants, or flowers to create a relaxing environment.

- **Schedule consistently:** A regular routine signals the transition into mindfulness practice and primes the mind-body for relaxation.

- **Model mindfulness:** Demonstrate mindfulness in your own life. Children learn through observing you.

- **Offer praise:** Provide specific, positive feedback when you notice mindful behaviors. This motivates consistency.

Making adjustments to set children up for success ensures they will look forward to mindfulness practice as special "them time" rather than see it as a chore.

CREATIVE MINDFULNESS ACTIVITIES FOR FAMILIES

Here we will explore engaging mindfulness games and practices that allow children to connect with mindfulness in a fun way while also building family bonds. Feel free to get creative in adapting or expanding on these activities!

. . .

Gratitude Games

- At bedtime or dinnertime, take turns sharing something you feel grateful for from that day. See who can come up with the most unique reasons for gratitude!

Five Senses Exploration

- Sit together in nature and see who can notice the most interesting sights, smells, textures, and sounds. Allow time to discuss observations.

Mindful Movement

- Take turns leading simple yoga poses or stretches focused on body awareness and coordinating breath with movement. Keep it lively!

Soothing Music

- Play calming instrumental music and give family members time to close their eyes and become fully immersed in the soundscape. Afterward, discuss feelings evoked and favorite elements.

Mindful Snack Time

- When enjoying a snack or meal, challenge each other to take three slow, mindful bites before continuing to eat. Savor flavors fully.

Heartfulness Practice

- Sit in a circle and take turns sending silent wishes of compassion (such as "I hope you have a great day") to each family member. See who can share the most heartfelt intentions.

Walking Meditation
  - Go for a slow, mindful walk together, focusing on the sensations in your feet and legs as you move. Observe sights and sounds while remaining anchored in your body.

MINDFUL BREATHING EXERCISE

• Find a comfortable seating position and guide each family member to silently count their breaths, numbering from 1 to 5 during both inhalation and exhalation. Practice this for a few cycles, anchoring attention solely on the rhythm of the breath.

As you introduce these activities, allow children to guide the experience, choosing variations or modifications that resonate with them. These initial steps lay the foundation – nurturing creativity and familiarity will foster continued enthusiasm and participation.

JOURNEY INTO MINDFULNESS THROUGH POETRY

Verses for Nurturing Presence in Young Hearts

Integrating poetry into a child's life enhances their sense of mindfulness and strengthens their bond with language. Poetic words, be they age-old classics, modern expressions, or delightful rhymes, expand their cognitive horizons, presenting a tapestry of emotions, ideas, and imagery. Here are some poems curated to foster peace and introspection for the young and curious. Each verse acts as a beacon to the present moment and a path to deeper understanding.

Verses for Young Explorers of Mindfulness:
- **Breath's Whisper**

> "Each breath taken, a silent prayer,
> Drawing essence from the boundless air.
> Each breath released, a subtle sea,
> Reflecting the tranquility we seek."

- **Nature's Soft Murmurs**

> "Amidst the gentle songs of trees,
> Lies wisdom, soft as a breeze.
> Stay rooted, stay here, and you might find,
> The wonders that nature has intertwined."

- **Between Moments**

> "In the space where moments interlink,
> Lies a world on the very brink.
> Delve deep, stay quiet, let thoughts flow free,
> And discover a haven, a sanctuary."

Rhymes to Ground Awareness:
- **Dawn's Gentle Embrace**

> "With a tender touch, the sun emerges,
> Weaving tales as the day surges.
> In these quiet dawns as day unfolds,
> Cherish the stories that the light holds."

- **Lunar Lullaby**

  > "In its gentle glow, the moon stands tall,
  > Guarding dreams, big and small.
  > Stay attuned to night's gentle tune,
  > With each melody, our spirits balloon."

Timeless Verses for Contemplation:
- **Waltz of the Foliage**

  > "Leaves dance, in a rhythmic spree,
  > Spiraling, spinning, as wild and free.
  > With each movement, each graceful slide,
  > Seek inner harmony, let tranquility guide."

- **Tales of the Stream**

  > "With intent, the river winds and bends,
  > Sharing stories that never end.
  > In its currents, wisdom does abound,
  > Here and now, that's where bliss is found."

Poems for New Minds on a Mindful Journey:
  Breath of Life

  > "Every breath in, a silent wish,
  > Drawing life from the vast abyss.
  > Every breath out, a gentle wave,
  > Echoing the peace we crave."

- **Whispers of Nature**

> "In the quiet hum of the trees,
> There's a lesson, a gentle tease.
> Be still, be present, and you'll see,
> The magic in a buzzing bee."

- **Moments in Between**

> "What lies between the tick and tock?
> A world of wonder, a secret dock.
> Dive in, be still, let your mind roam,
> Find in that silence, a way back home."

Rhymes to Anchor Awareness:
The Sun's Gentle Rise

> "Glowing softly, the sun does rise,
> Painting stories in morning skies.
> Quiet moments, as day does start,
> Hold them gently, close to your heart."

- **Moon's Silvery Beam**

> "Glimmering, shimmering, moon's soft glow,
> Watching over, as dreams below.
> Be present, in night's sweet song,
> With each note, we grow strong."

Enduring Verses for Pausing and Reflecting:
- **Dance of the Leaves**

> "Leaves rustle, in a gentle prance,

> Swirling, twirling, in nature's dance.
> With each flutter, and sway, and glide,
> Find your center, let peace reside."

- **River's Journey**

> "River winds, with purpose so clear,
> Whispering tales, for those who'd hear.
> In its flow, a lesson profound,
> Be in the moment, that's where joy's found."

Encourage your child to dive into these verses, feeling each word and its rhythm. Read with intention, highlighting the beauty of language, and let the poems become a starting point for discussions on mindfulness. Immerse in these poetic journeys and unlock the serenity within.

CHAPTER 15
GAMES FOR CHILDREN TO LEARN MEDITATION
GAMES AND ACTIVITIES TO TEACH CHILDREN MEDITATION TECHNIQUES:

LEARNING meditation and mindfulness at a young age can provide children with invaluable skills for life. When practiced regularly, these techniques help kids build concentration, reduce stress, and cultivate compassion. Luckily, meditation doesn't have to be a dull or difficult endeavor for children. Creative games and activities can make learning meditation fun and engaging.

MINDFUL COLORING

A simple yet effective way to introduce mindful meditation to kids is through mindful coloring. This activity helps direct a child's attention to the present moment. The repetitive motion of coloring acts as an "anchor" for their awareness. As children move the crayon across the page, they learn to tune into the sensory aspects of the activity – the feel of the crayon in their hand, the sound it makes scraping across the paper, the visual complexity of the patterns. If their mind starts to drift, they gently return their focus to the coloring. Over time, they build concentration skills and the ability to pay attention to the here and now.

Set up a coloring station with a variety of coloring books and a rainbow of crayon choices. Instruct children to start coloring slowly, noticing the textures and colors on the page. Encourage them to focus on keeping their mind in the present, fully immersed in the creative process. If thoughts arise, gently return focus to the coloring activity. For an added mindfulness component, have kids color symmetrical or repeating patterns. The methodical symmetry helps anchor attention and provides satisfaction when completed. After finishing the coloring session, discuss how they felt during the activity. Did their mood change? Could they maintain focus throughout? Coloring is an introductory mindfulness exercise kids can practice anytime.

MINDFUL MOVEMENT

Children naturally love to move and play. Mindful movement activities harness this energy in a positive way. These games use physical activity as an anchor for a child's attention in the moment. Simple movements are repeated over and over, emphasizing body awareness and control. As kids engage in repetitive motions, their focus shifts inward. For a brief time, they experience moving mindfully, without distractions or judgment. The goal is not perfect execution of the movements but rather conscious focus and direction of the mind.

One fun mindful movement activity is a "balancing challenge." Have children try balancing on one foot, walking heel-to-toe in a straight line, rolling a ball from hand to hand, or carrying an object across the room and back. Challenge them to complete these actions as slowly and carefully as possible. Encourage concentration on body sensations and movement. If the mind wanders, redirect attention to the balancing task at hand. Start with short, simple challenges and then advance to more complex, longer balancing tasks. In the end, discuss how they directed their focus and found balance and control in their movements and minds.

MINDFUL BREATHING WITH IMAGERY

Simple breathing exercises form the core foundation of mindfulness meditation. Paired with guided imagery, kids can embark on mindful journeys that spark creativity and focus their attention. Provide a vivid narrative that describes an imaginary world, ideally one with calming natural elements – like a lake, mountain, or forest. Instruct children to envision themselves in this peaceful setting while steadily breathing in and out. Guide them to imagine sights, sounds, and sensations that create a detailed experience in their mind's eye. This mental role-play combines storytelling with purposeful breathing. Regular practice strengthens their ability to concentrate and visualize. Kids learn they can return to this calming inner world anytime simply by taking mindful breaths.

Start by having kids sit comfortably with eyes closed or in a soft gaze. Offer guidance in slow, steady breathing – deep inhale through the nose, long exhale through the mouth. Once settled, describe entry into the peaceful setting – walking into a forest, diving into a lake, climbing a mountain trail. Fill the journey with multi-sensory details. Notice changes in breathing and alertness. Afterward, discuss their impressions of the visualized world. Was it vivid and engaging? Did their mood change? Over time, let the kids lead, describing their own imaginary journeys while breathing mindfully.

SOOTHING MUSIC AND MINDFUL LISTENING

Music, when listened to attentively, can facilitate mindfulness and relaxation. Have children lie down and close their eyes while you play soft instrumental music. Ask them to bring full attention to the sounds they hear. Notice ranges in tone, volume, rhythm, and melody. Without judgment, let the music wash over them and elicit different feelings and sensations. Kids may visualize colors or scenery that complement the soundscape. If thoughts intrude, gently return focus to mindful listening. Afterward, reflect on the experience of conscious, focused listening. Was it calming? Did it enhance mood and creativity? This activity trains the ability to attune awareness and find serenity through music.

For extra engagement, provide percussive instruments like drums, xylophones, or rain sticks. Encourage mindful listening while also following along through playing. Add different actions, like tapping feet or fingers to the beat. The goal remains to anchor full attention to the sound and music, practicing mindfulness in an interactive way.

RELAXING BODY SCANS

Body scan meditations are attention-focusing exercises that cultivate awareness of physical sensations. Lying still, children tune into feelings in different body parts, systematically scanning from head to toe. This builds concentration skills while eliciting relaxation. Kids remain engaged as they explore inner perceptions of their bodies. Release stored tension by tensing and relaxing muscle groups. Visualize calming sensations like warmth and heaviness replacing stress and discomfort.

Guide children into a comfortable resting position, either seated or lying down. Instruct them to close their eyes and breathe steadily. Starting from the top of the head, bring focus to discernable sensations – heat, pulsing, tightness, aching. Scan downward through muscle groups, spending several slow breaths at each area. Provide intermittent prompts to relax, release, or restore feelings of warmth and calm. Adapt any sensory language based on a child's response. For example, "imagine sending waves of relaxation from your toes up through your body." End the session by discussing their experiences and sensations. With regular practice, body scans effectively reduce anxiety and stress levels.

MINDFULNESS THROUGH NATURE

Nature-based activities provide multisensory experiences that grab children's attention and focus their awareness on the present. Take kids on mindful nature walks or treasure hunts outdoors. Have them notice sensory details – bird songs, rustling leaves, fragrant flowers. Feel the warmth of the sun, the breeze on their skin. Encourage curiosity and appreciation for natural wonders, large and small. Lie outside and watch clouds drift by. Guide children to zoom in their attention on minute details, then zoom out to broader awareness of surroundings. If thoughts arise, gently return focus to the direct sensory experience. Afterward, reflect on their observations, sensations, and emotions. Discuss how mindfully engaging with nature differed from a walk preoccupied with inner thoughts and worries. Make connections between breathing meditations and the sights and sounds that elicited calm. Outdoor mindfulness activities not only increase concentration but also foster caring for the environment.

CREATIVE ARTS AND CRAFTS

Arts and crafts projects provide sensory-rich, focused activities ideal for cultivating mindfulness. Coloring, sculpting with clay, beadwork, origami, collage making – each absorbs a child's attention fully on the creative process. Encourage an open, non-judging attitude. Don't worry about perfection. Instead, guide children to mindfully observe textures, colors, and shapes. Immerse in the sensations of folding, rolling, cutting, gluing, and painting. If the mind drifts, return gently to sensory engagement in the art-making. Display finished creations as reminders to live mindfully, appreciating the beauty of everyday moments.

For musical artistry, provide simple percussion instruments like maracas, claves, and bells. Instruct children to mindfully play, noticing sound qualities and rhythmic patterns. Alternatively, play relaxing music during art time. Consciously focus attention on the melodies and harmonies while immersed in creative work. Dance or move to the music mindfully. Feel the beat resonate physically. Allow the music to enhance the sensory experience of the arts and crafts activity. Creativity flows freely when anchored in mindful awareness of each passing moment.

PRACTICING KINDNESS THROUGH COMPASSION MEDITATION

Incorporating compassion and kindness into meditation practice helps children cultivate empathy and connection. Guide kids to send well wishes through their breaths. Breathe in warmth, joy, and happiness. Exhale compassion, care, and concern to loved ones, friends, or even strangers. Visualize this energy spreading outwards, flowing endlessly. Practice regularly to strengthen feelings of empathy and human connection.

Another compassion-based mindfulness activity is imagining loved ones. Instruct children to picture family or friends in their minds while breathing slowly. Visualize giving and receiving warmth, care, and appreciation. Send silent gratitude to those they hold dear. Or picture people in challenging life circumstances. Breathe compassion towards their struggles. Imagine easing emotional or physical suffering. This heart-centered meditation fosters altruism, care for others, and a sense of common humanity. Guide children to carry this spirit of compassion into their daily lives.

GUIDED RELAXATION AND VISUALIZATION

Relaxation activities and guided visualization soothe the nervous system and calm the mind. Have children get into a relaxed, seated position and close their eyes. In a soft, steady voice, describe calming sensations washing over the body from head to toe. Use imagery like warm sunshine filling the body with heaviness and peace. Or ripples of relaxation flowing through the muscles. Adapt suggestions to focus on releasing tension, quieting thoughts, and finding tranquility. For variety, guide kids to visualize images like lying in a grassy meadow or floating on gentle ocean waves. These calming inner visions elicit a relaxation response. Practice guided relaxation sessions regularly to relieve stress, improve sleep quality and boost overall well-being. Afterward, discuss their experiences. Did they feel relaxed, heavy, or warm? Were they able to visualize suggested images? Did distracting thoughts decrease? Track progress in mastering mind-body relaxation through routine guided practice.

RELAXATION THROUGH SQUEEZING MUSCLES

Progressive muscle relaxation teaches children to identify and release body tension through systematic tensing and releasing of muscle groups. Guide kids to take slow breaths and squeeze or tighten targeted areas for several seconds – hands, arms, legs, abdomen, back, shoulders, and face. Then exhale, abruptly relaxing the tensed muscles. Have them notice sensations as the tension melts away. Repeat with other muscle groups, eventually tensing and releasing the whole body. Conclude with resting in a calm, relaxed state. The contrast of tension and release brings awareness to physical stress and the ability to consciously relax both body and mind. This exercise doubles as a body scan activity, building focus and mindfulness of internal sensations. Practice regularly to reduce chronic stress and anxiety levels.

MINDFULNESS GAMES AND EXERCISES

Playful, interactive games provide lighthearted ways to learn mindfulness skills. Sing songs that describe mindful actions like brushing teeth, washing dishes, or petting animals. Make mindfulness-themed crafts like glitter jars to watch settle when emotions are strong. Water plants or walk pets mindfully, noticing detailed sensory experiences. Practice mindful eating by slowly nibbling a piece of chocolate, noticing flavors, textures, and aroma. Make a listening game where kids close their eyes and identify everyday sounds. The possibilities are endless for inventing mindful games or adding a mindfulness twist to existing pastimes. The key is keeping activities simple, sensory-based, and anchored in the present moment. Playfulness and fun remove resistance to meditation, allowing kids to absorb mindfulness skills more organically.

MINDFULNESS MEDITATION WITH PEERS

Children often find meditation more engaging as a shared experience. Organize group mindfulness sessions for kids to practice together. Set up stations for mindful coloring, movement, or nature activities. Lead collective breathing practices. Sit in a circle for body scans or guided relaxation. Tell mindfulness-themed stories. Set an intention as a group to pay attention to the present moment non-judgmentally. Then discuss experiences as peers. Children will feed off each other's insights, creativity, and focus. Establishing a supportive community of mindfulness practice builds motivation and accountability. Kids see how their friends integrate meditation into daily life, encouraging regular practice. And they have fun learning mindfulness as a team!

The benefits of teaching children meditation and mindfulness practices are tremendous. But learning takes patience, practice, and an array of creative techniques. Make meditation varied, interactive, and playful. Celebrate small successes and moments of conscious awareness. With regular practice, kids build life-long skills for focusing attention, relieving stress, and accessing inner peace. Guide them on this journey with compassion, flexibility, and an ever-open heart.

MEDITATION MAGIC: A FAMILY'S PATH TO PEACE AND HAPPINESS

STORYTIME:

© 2023 Foss Plus. All rights reserved.

The Wilson Family's Meditation Adventure

It was a typical busy Saturday morning in the Wilson household. In the kitchen, 12-year-old Zoe and 10-year-old Noah were scarfing down pancakes drenched in syrup. Upstairs, their parents, Jenny and Dan, were scrambling to get ready for the day.

"Hurry up and eat, kids!"

Called Jenny as she raced down the stairs, still pulling her hair up in a ponytail.

> "We've got a full day ahead - Zoe, you have dance class, Noah, you have basketball practice, and then we need to go grocery shopping."

The kids let out twin groans, already feeling exhausted just thinking about their packed schedules.

> "Do we have to go to all our activities today?"

Protested Zoe.

> "I'd rather just hang out with my friends."

Noah nodded in agreement, mouth full of pancakes.

> "Can I skip basketball and go to Jason's house to play video games?"

Jenny sighed, knowing how overbooked her kids felt. She and Dan had been discussing ways to help Zoe and Noah manage their stress and just enjoy being kids. Suddenly, she had an idea.

> "How about we do something different today?"

Jenny proposed.

> "Let's have a family meditation adventure instead!"

Zoe and Noah's eyes widened in surprise. Meditation sounded about as fun as going to the doctor.

Seeing their hesitation, Jenny quickly added,

> "It'll be a cool mindfulness game day! Dad and I will show you how meditation can be playful."

Now the kids looked curious. Noah asked,

> "What kind of games?"

> "You'll see!"

Teased Dan as he entered the kitchen.

> "Trust us, by the end of today, you'll be begging to meditate."

After canceling their obligations, the Wilsons changed into comfy athleisure clothes and met in the living room. Jenny and Dan had moved the furniture aside and laid out yoga mats and pillows.

> "Let's start with a body scan meditation."

Explained Dan.

> "Lie down and close your eyes. Focus on your breathing."

As the family tuned into their breath, Jenny continued guiding them.

> "Now imagine you have a magical scanner that can detect any tension in your body. Let's slowly scan from head to toe."

The Wilsons mentally scanned their bodies, noticing areas of tightness and consciously relaxing them. Noah smiled as the tension dissipated from his shoulders. Zoe realized she had been furrowing her brow and was able to smooth it out.

After finishing the scan, Jenny asked,

> "So, how was that?"

> "It felt like a scan at the doctor's office, but in a good way."

Remarked Noah.

> "My body feels looser now."

> "Yeah, I didn't realize how scrunched up I was until the scan showed me where to relax."

Added Zoe.
Dan high-fived them.

> "Awesome job! Let's try another meditation."

The kids sat up eagerly. They were surprised to find the simple scanning exercise so calming.

> "This one is called the Fortune Teller."

Said, Jenny.

> "Imagine yourself visiting a mystical fortune teller. What questions would you ask about your future?"

Zoe and Noah closed their eyes, envisioning walking into a candlelit tent draped with shiny fabrics. Sitting at a table covered in tarot cards and crystals was a woman in flowing, colorful robes.

Zoe asked the fortune teller about her future dreams and career. In her mind, the fortune teller replied,

> "You will find great success if you follow your passions."

Noah questioned the fortune teller about his future family.

> "I see much love and laughter ahead."

She responded.

> "Cherish each moment."

After several minutes of imaginary fortune-telling, Jenny's voice brought them back.

> "What did you ask the fortune teller?"

The kids described their visions excitedly. Just pretending to glimpse the future left them feeling lighter and more optimistic.

> "Very cool!"

Said Dan.

> "Meditations, where you visualize, can really spark your imagination."

The family did a few more guided meditations, including a mountain hike and a beach vacation. With each new journey, Zoe and Noah sank deeper into tranquility. Time seemed to slow down.

After the last meditation, the kids stayed still, eyes closed, cherishing the inner peace. Finally, Zoe spoke up.

> "That was seriously the most relaxing morning ever. My mind feels so clear now."

> "I know."

Noah agreed.

> "Can we do meditation every weekend from now on?"

Jenny and Dan chuckled, exchanging a knowing glance.

> "We thought you'd come around to it!"

Said, Jenny.

> "For sure, kids."

Replied Dan.

> "We're so glad you gave it a chance."

From then on, family meditation time simply became part of the Wilsons' routine, a new shared ritual they all looked forward to. Some weekends they went on visual journeys - deep sea diving, jungle safaris, or trips to outer space. Other times they did body scans or fortune teller meditations.

Noah found that a quick meditation before basketball helped him focus and stay centered under pressure. Zoe used mindful breathing techniques before auditions and performances to calm her stage fright.

On hectic weekday mornings, the whole family would pause for a short mindfulness exercise together before heading out the door. It became their port in the storm, a way to reconnect before being pulled into the day's activities.

Over time, the kids came to treasure their meditation adventures with Mom and Dad. They realized that just 15 minutes of guided meditation could make their whole day feel less stressed and more magical. It was like hitting a mental reset button.

Beyond simply feeling calmer and more resilient, the shared practice brought their family closer together. Laughter often echoed through the house as they embarked on silly imaginary quests. And a sense of connection lingered long after their meditations ended.

Zoe and Noah now saw mindfulness as an adventure rather than a chore. And they had their parents to thank for showing them how joyful and transformative it could be. They realized that meditation was a gift they could carry with them for life.

As Jenny often said at the end of their sessions, hands joined:

> "May we take this mindful magic into the world today with open hearts and minds."

The End.

PART 5: ESTABLISHING MINDFULNESS AS A LIFESTYLE

Overcoming Hurdles in Teaching Meditation to Children.
Teaching Meditation to Children from Diverse Cultures

CHAPTER 16
OVERCOMING HURDLES IN TEACHING MEDITATION TO CHILDREN

TEACHING meditation to children can be quite a challenge. Children may push back against the practice or struggle to grasp its concepts. In this chapter, we will explore the common obstacles faced by parents and caregivers when introducing meditation to children. Fear not! We will also provide you with valuable tips and strategies to conquer these hurdles and make meditation an enjoyable experience for children.

THE RESISTANCE BATTLE

Children often resist meditation for various reasons. They may find it dull, uncomfortable, or simply too perplexing to comprehend. However, there are effective methods to overcome this resistance and bring children into the realm of meditation.

To conquer the resistance obstacle, parents and caregivers can infuse meditation with elements of excitement and delight. Transforming the practice into a game, weaving captivating stories, or engaging in fun activities can all make meditation more appealing to children. As they embark on this journey, they can visualize themselves as brave explorers venturing into a world of serenity and tranquility. With eyes closed, they can imagine strolling through a magical forest, where they hear the whispering leaves and the cheerful songs of birds. Each step brings them closer to a place of inner peace and calm.

As the meditation session progresses, parents and caregivers can craft enchanting tales, whisking children away to imaginary lands. These tales may involve noble dragons residing in mystical castles or dolphins guiding them through the depths of their own minds in underwater kingdoms. By blending storytelling with meditation, children's imagination will ignite, fostering a sense of wonder and active engagement.

CONFRONTING DISCOMFORT

Another hurdle in teaching meditation to children is physical discomfort. Sitting still for extended periods can lead to restlessness and discomfort. However, fret not! We have an answer.

Introducing movement-based meditation techniques, such as yoga, can effectively address this challenge. Yoga blends gentle movements with deep breathing, providing children with an interactive and dynamic way to embrace mindfulness. Picture a group of children forming animal poses, emulating the strength of lions, elephants, or even the graceful slithering of snakes. Each pose becomes a gateway to self-awareness and relaxation. By intertwining physical movements with mindful breathing, children establish harmony between their bodies and minds. Not only does this approach alleviate discomfort, but it also allows children to joyfully connect with their bodies in a profound way.

UNDERSTANDING THE ABSTRACT

Understanding the abstract nature of meditation can be perplexing for children. Mindfulness and awareness concepts may seem too intangible or elusive to grasp. Don't worry, for there are ways to bridge this gap and help children embrace meditation.

Parents and caregivers can simplify the language and employ concrete metaphors to make meditation more relatable. Imagine explaining mindfulness to a child by comparing it to a blossoming flower. You could describe how, just as a flower requires sunlight and water to thrive, our minds need attention and care to flourish. By nurturing our minds through meditation, we can cultivate happiness and resilience, much like tending to a garden.

Visual aids can also play a vital role in meditation sessions. Using vibrant illustrations or simple diagrams, parents and caregivers can depict the breath, the mind, and the various sensations experienced during meditation. These visual representations serve as anchors, helping children grasp abstract concepts and establish a tangible connection to their inner experiences.

By addressing the challenges of resistance, discomfort, and comprehension, parents and caregivers can create an environment that nurtures and supports children in their meditation practice. Through playful engagement, movement-based techniques, and relatable metaphors, children can embark on a transformative journey toward inner peace and self-discovery.

In the subsequent chapters, we will delve deeper into specific strategies and activities, offering a plethora of tools to help you overcome these challenges. Embrace your creativity, adapt to the unique needs of each child, and unlock the infinite potential within them. Together, we will create a path toward a lifetime of mindfulness, resilience, and well-being.

OVERCOMING OBSTACLES IN TEACHING MEDITATION TO CHILDREN

Teaching meditation to children can present its fair share of challenges. Some children resist the practice, finding it tedious or unappealing. Others struggle with discomfort during meditation, feeling restless or physically uneasy. Additionally, the complexity of meditation concepts can pose difficulties for young minds to grasp. In this chapter, we will explore these common hurdles and offer practical strategies for parents and caregivers to overcome them, ensuring a positive and enriching meditation experience for children.

CONQUERING RESISTANCE

Resistance to meditation can manifest in various ways, and boredom is a frequent culprit. Children may perceive meditation as monotonous or lacking excitement, leading them to resist participation. To combat this, parents and caregivers can infuse meditation with elements of playfulness and creativity.

. . .

Incorporating games, stories, or imaginative exercises into meditation sessions can capture children's interest and make the practice more engaging. For example, a guided meditation that transports children on a captivating imaginary adventure can kindle their curiosity and enhance their enjoyment of the experience. By introducing meditation in a manner that aligns with children's natural inclinations and interests, resistance can transform into enthusiasm.

ADDRESSING DISCOMFORT

Physical discomfort is another challenge that may deter children from embracing meditation. Sitting still for extended periods or assuming specific postures can lead to restlessness or bodily discomfort. To alleviate this obstacle, parents and caregivers can make adjustments to ensure the child's physical comfort during meditation.

Providing cushions or alternative seating options that support the child's body can help alleviate discomfort. Encouraging children to find a posture that feels natural and relaxed, such as sitting on a chair or even lying down if needed, can make the practice more accessible and enjoyable. By attending to physical comfort, parents and caregivers create an environment that encourages children to fully engage in meditation without hindrance.

SIMPLIFYING COMPLEXITY

The abstract nature of meditation can present challenges for children, making it difficult for them to comprehend and engage in the practice. Concepts like mindfulness and quieting the mind may seem daunting or confusing to young minds. Lengthy or intricate meditation techniques can overwhelm children and hinder their enthusiasm for meditation.

To overcome this hurdle, parents and caregivers should start with simple and concise meditation sessions. Introduce basic techniques that are easy for children to understand and apply, such as focusing on the breath or observing sensations in the body. By breaking down meditation into manageable components, children can grasp the fundamental concepts and gradually expand their practice. As their understanding and confidence grow, parents and caregivers can gradually introduce more advanced techniques and extend the duration of meditation sessions, ensuring a gradual and steady progression.

By recognizing and addressing the reasons behind resistance, discomfort, and complexity, parents and caregivers can empower children to embrace meditation and reap its numerous benefits. Through playful engagement, physical comfort, and gradual progression, children can embark on a transformative journey of self-discovery and inner peace. In the following chapters, we will delve deeper into specific strategies and activities, equipping you with the tools to guide children through these challenges successfully.

UNLOCKING THE POWER OF MEDITATION FOR CHILDREN

Teaching meditation to children can be an exciting journey filled with discovery and growth. However, it's not uncommon to encounter resistance along the way. In this chapter, we will explore effective strategies to overcome resistance, create engaging meditation experiences, and cultivate a supportive environment for children to thrive.

THE PATH OF ENGAGEMENT

To overcome resistance, we must make meditation a captivating and interactive experience for children. By infusing elements of play, creativity, and imagination, we can unlock their curiosity and enthusiasm. Engaging in meditation activities that involve storytelling, visualization exercises, or interactive games can transform the practice into an adventure that captures children's attention.

Guided meditations designed specifically for children offer another powerful tool for engagement. These meditations use age-appropriate language, themes, and storytelling techniques that resonate with young minds. By immersing children in a vivid narrative, guided meditations ignite their imagination and foster a sense of wonder, making the practice both enjoyable and captivating.

THE JOURNEY OF PROGRESSION

Introducing meditation to children requires a gradual approach. Starting with short and simple sessions allows children to ease into the practice without feeling overwhelmed. It is essential to create a foundation of positive experiences that build confidence and familiarity with meditation.

As children become more comfortable and receptive, parents and caregivers can gradually increase the duration and complexity of the meditation sessions. This gentle progression nurtures the growth of their meditation skills, ensuring that they continue to engage with the practice in a way that feels natural and empowering.

THE POWER OF COMMUNITY

Creating a supportive environment is crucial for children to overcome resistance and embrace meditation wholeheartedly. Practicing meditation as a family or within a group of peers establishes a sense of community and shared experience. When children witness their loved ones or friends engaging in meditation, it reinforces the significance of the practice and inspires them to participate.

Open and honest communication between parents, caregivers, and children is essential. Encouraging children to express their thoughts, concerns, and challenges regarding meditation creates a safe space for them to be heard and understood. By addressing their needs and providing guidance, we can nurture their trust and motivation to continue on their meditation journey.

In this chapter, we have explored powerful strategies to overcome resistance, engage children in meditation, and cultivate a supportive environment. By infusing playfulness, gradually progressing the practice, and fostering a sense of community, we empower children to unlock the transformative benefits of meditation. In the upcoming chapters, we will delve deeper into specific techniques and activities that will further enhance their meditation experiences. Together, we will nurture a generation of mindful, resilient, and fulfilled children.

UNLEASHING THE POWER OF MEDITATION FOR CHILDREN

As children embrace meditation and overcome resistance, they unlock a wealth of benefits that enrich their lives and nurture their growth. In this chapter, we will explore the remarkable advantages of meditation for children, ranging from emotional well-being to cognitive development and social skills.

EMBRACING EMOTIONAL WELL-BEING

Meditation serves as a powerful tool for developing emotional intelligence and promoting overall emotional well-being in children. Through meditation, children gain the ability to recognize and understand their emotions, fostering self-awareness. By cultivating this awareness, children can better regulate their emotions, navigate stress, anxiety, and negative feelings, and find inner balance. With continued practice, meditation empowers children to cultivate a profound sense of calm, tranquility, and resilience.

BOOSTING COGNITIVE DEVELOPMENT

Regular meditation practice contributes to the cognitive development of children, enhancing their mental abilities and academic performance. By sharpening their focus, attention, and concentration, meditation equips children with the skills to excel in their studies and absorb knowledge more effectively. Moreover, meditation nurtures memory and cognitive flexibility, enabling children to adapt to new challenges and problem-solving situations with confidence and ease. Through meditation, children unlock the limitless potential of their minds, fostering a foundation for lifelong learning and growth.

FOSTERING SOCIAL SKILLS

In addition to its individual benefits, meditation plays a crucial role in the development of children's social skills. By cultivating qualities such as empathy, compassion, and kindness, meditation empowers children to build and maintain positive relationships with others. As children learn to listen attentively, respect differences, and respond with empathy, they become more effective communicators and collaborators. The foundation of social skills established through meditation creates a harmonious and inclusive environment for children to thrive, fostering a sense of connection and community.

THE JOURNEY CONTINUES

As children embark on their meditation journey, the benefits of emotional well-being, cognitive development, and social skills intertwine, creating a tapestry of growth and flourishing. Through regular practice, children cultivate a deep understanding of their emotions, harness their mental capabilities, and embrace harmonious relationships with those around them. The power of meditation unlocks a world of possibilities, empowering children to navigate life's challenges with grace and resilience.

In the upcoming chapters, we will delve deeper into specific techniques, mindfulness exercises, and creative activities that will enhance children's meditation experiences and maximize the benefits they reap. Together, we will continue to explore the transformative potential of meditation, empowering children to lead fulfilling lives infused with mindfulness, compassion, and joy.

NURTURING HARMONY IN TEACHING MEDITATION TO CHILDREN

In the pursuit of teaching meditation to children, it is crucial to address potential power imbalances that may arise. By fostering collaboration and maintaining a positive approach, parents and caregivers can create an environment where children feel empowered and respected. In this chapter, we will explore strategies to address power imbalances, ensuring that the practice of meditation is approached with harmony and mutual understanding.

CULTIVATING COLLABORATION

To avoid power imbalances, it is essential to view meditation as a collaborative practice rather than enforcing it as a form of discipline; parents and caregivers should involve children in decision-making and encourage their active participation. By giving children a sense of agency and choice, they feel respected and valued.

When introducing meditation, engage children in open conversations about their thoughts, feelings, and preferences. Allow them to express their ideas and concerns, ensuring that their voices are heard. By actively involving children in the process, parents and caregivers foster a collaborative atmosphere where both parties contribute to the development and evolution of the meditation practice.

MODELING POSITIVE PRACTICES

Parents and caregivers play a vital role in shaping children's perception of meditation. To avoid power imbalances, it is crucial to model meditation as a positive and peaceful practice. Instead of using it as a form of punishment or control, demonstrate the personal benefits of meditation and the joy it brings.

Make meditation a shared experience by practicing it together as a family or with other children. This collective approach reinforces the idea that meditation is a valuable and enjoyable activity for everyone involved. By embodying a positive and peaceful mindset during meditation, parents and caregivers inspire children to view it as a source of tranquility and personal growth.

CREATING A SAFE SPACE

Establishing a safe and nurturing environment is paramount to addressing power imbalances in teaching meditation. Ensure that children feel comfortable expressing their thoughts, concerns, and emotions freely. Encourage open communication and actively listen to their perspectives, valuing their input.

When conflicts or challenges arise, approach them with empathy and understanding. Seek resolution through dialogue and negotiation, fostering a sense of mutual respect and cooperation. By creating a safe space where children feel valued and heard, parents and caregivers can cultivate an atmosphere of harmony and trust, promoting a positive relationship with meditation.

In this chapter, we have explored strategies to address power imbalances when teaching meditation to children. By embracing collaboration, modeling positive practices, and creating a safe space, parents and caregivers can foster an environment that empowers children and nurtures their well-being. As we move forward, we will continue to discover ways to ensure that meditation remains a transformative and inclusive practice for all children.

RESISTANCE TO MEDITATION: ADDRESSING POWER IMBALANCES

Nurturing Harmony in Teaching Meditation to Children

In our journey to teach meditation to children, it's important to address power imbalances that may arise. By promoting collaboration and cultivating a positive approach, parents and caregivers can create an environment where children feel empowered and respected. In this chapter, we will explore strategies to address power imbalances, ensuring that meditation is embraced willingly and wholeheartedly.

THE COLLABORATIVE PATH

To overcome resistance and foster harmony, it is crucial to view meditation as a collaborative practice. Rather than imposing it as a disciplinary measure, parents and caregivers should involve children in the decision-making process and encourage their active participation. By giving children a sense of agency and choice, they feel valued and respected.

When introducing meditation, engage children in open conversations, allowing them to express their thoughts, feelings, and preferences. Emphasize the importance of their input and create an environment where their voices are heard. By actively involving children in the practice, parents and caregivers foster collaboration, where both parties contribute to the development and evolution of the meditation experience.

Modeling Positivity

Parents and caregivers play a significant role in shaping children's perception of meditation. To address power imbalances, it is essential to model meditation as a positive and peaceful experience. Instead of using it as a tool for control or punishment, showcase the personal benefits and joy it brings.

Make meditation a shared experience by practicing it together as a family or with other children. Embody a positive and peaceful mindset during meditation, demonstrating its value and the calm it can bring. By doing so, parents and caregivers inspire children to view meditation as a source of tranquility and personal growth rather than something imposed upon them.

Creating a Safe Haven

Creating a safe and nurturing environment is paramount in addressing power imbalances during meditation. Ensure that children feel comfortable expressing their thoughts, concerns, and emotions freely. Encourage open communication and actively listen to their perspectives, validating their input.

When conflicts or challenges arise, approach them with empathy and understanding. Seek resolution through dialogue and negotiation, fostering mutual respect and cooperation. By creating a safe haven where children feel valued and heard, parents and caregivers cultivate an atmosphere of harmony and trust, allowing meditation to be embraced willingly and authentically.

In this chapter, we have explored strategies to address power imbalances in teaching meditation to children. By promoting collaboration, modeling positivity, and creating a safe haven, parents and caregivers empower children to overcome resistance and discover the transformative benefits of meditation on their own terms. As we continue our journey, we will delve deeper into specific techniques and activities that further nurture the relationship between children and meditation, fostering a lifelong practice of well-being and self-discovery.

COERCION AND MANIPULATION: FOSTERING RESISTANCE

Nurturing Harmony in Teaching Meditation to Children

In our endeavor to teach meditation to children, we must be mindful of potential power imbalances that can lead to resistance. When parents or caregivers use meditation as a tool for control or punishment, children may naturally resist in their pursuit of autonomy. These power dynamics can evoke feelings of resentment and defiance, hindering the child's willingness to embrace meditation. To create a healthy and positive relationship with meditation, it is crucial to acknowledge and address these power imbalances.

Recognizing Coercion and Manipulation

When meditation is imposed upon children as a means of

control or punishment, it erodes their sense of autonomy and free will. Children have an innate desire for independence and the ability to make choices that align with their own values and interests. When meditation becomes associated with coercion or manipulation, resistance is likely to emerge as a defense mechanism.

Fostering Autonomy and Choice

To foster a healthy relationship with meditation, parents and caregivers must prioritize autonomy and choice. Instead of imposing meditation as a non-negotiable requirement, provide children with the opportunity to make decisions and have a say in their meditation practice.

Engage children in discussions about meditation, allowing them to express their thoughts and preferences. By offering choices, such as different meditation techniques or varying durations, children feel empowered and invested in their own practice. This collaborative approach nurtures a sense of ownership and encourages children to embrace meditation willingly.

Creating a Positive Framework

Shifting the perception of meditation from a tool of control to a positive and beneficial practice is key to overcoming resistance. Emphasize the inherent value of meditation for personal growth, well-being, and inner peace. Discuss the positive effects meditation can have on emotions, focus, and overall mental health.

Model a positive attitude towards meditation by incorporating it into your own routine. When children witness the benefits firsthand and observe the joy and calmness it brings, they are more likely to view meditation in a positive light. By creating a supportive and nurturing environment, children can associate meditation with positivity and willingly engage in the practice.

Building Trust and Connection

Addressing power imbalances requires building trust and connection between parents, caregivers, and children. Establish open lines of communication, actively listen to children's concerns, and validate their emotions and experiences. By demonstrating empathy and understanding, parents and caregivers can create a safe space for children to express their thoughts and feelings about meditation freely.

Resolve conflicts or disagreements through respectful dialogue, seeking common ground and compromise. By involving children in decision-making processes, they feel respected and valued, strengthening their connection with meditation.

In this chapter, we have explored strategies to address power imbalances in teaching meditation to children. By fostering autonomy, creating a positive framework, and building trust and connection, parents and caregivers can overcome resistance and nurture a healthy relationship between children and meditation. As we progress, we will delve deeper into specific techniques and activities that promote a harmonious and empowering meditation practice for children.

LACK OF AGENCY: NURTURING A SENSE OF EMPOWERMENT

Fostering Empowerment in Teaching Meditation to Children

In our quest to teach meditation to children, it is crucial to recognize the importance of empowering them and respecting their agency. When meditation is imposed upon children without considering their opinions or desires, it can lead to resistance and a sense of disempowerment. To overcome this, parents and caregivers must shift the narrative and involve children in the decision-making process. By giving children a voice and choice in their meditation practice, they can develop a sense of ownership and empowerment. In this chapter, we will explore strategies to address power imbalances, fostering a harmonious and empowering relationship with meditation.

Acknowledging Lack of Agency

Children, like adults, have an inherent need for agency and control over their lives. Imposing meditation without considering their opinions or desires can diminish their sense of empowerment. It is essential to recognize that children should have a say in their meditation practice to foster a positive and collaborative environment.

Shifting the Narrative

To overcome resistance, parents and caregivers should shift the narrative surrounding meditation. Instead of imposing it as an obligation or requirement, engage children in open discussions about their thoughts, preferences, and comfort levels. By inviting their input, children feel valued and respected, and their perspective on meditation shifts from something forced to something they have ownership over.

Involving Children in Decision-making

Empowering children through decision-making is crucial in cultivating a positive relationship with meditation. Provide opportunities for them to express their preferences, such as choosing the meditation technique, duration, or time of practice. By involving children in these decisions, they feel a sense of ownership and control, which enhances their willingness to engage in meditation voluntarily.

Encouraging Exploration and Adaptation

Each child is unique, and their preferences for meditation may vary. Encourage children to explore different meditation techniques, such as guided imagery, focused breathing, or body scans. Allow them to adapt and personalize their practice based on their individual needs and interests. By embracing their creativity and autonomy, children can develop a deeper connection with meditation and discover what resonates with them.

Embracing Flexibility and Consistency

Flexibility is essential when addressing power imbalances. While involving children in decision-making, it is crucial to maintain consistency in promoting a regular meditation practice. Establish a routine that suits their schedule and preferences while also reinforcing the importance of consistency. By striking a balance between flexibility and consistency, children feel a sense of empowerment within a structured framework.

. . .

In this chapter, we have explored strategies to address power imbalances in teaching meditation to children. By shifting the narrative, involving children in decision-making, encouraging exploration and adaptation, and embracing flexibility and consistency, parents and caregivers foster a sense of ownership and empowerment. As we move forward, we will delve deeper into specific techniques and activities that further nurture children's sense of agency and create a flourishing meditation practice that is uniquely their own.

COLLABORATIVE APPROACH: HONORING CHOICES AND PREFERENCES

To overcome power imbalances, it is crucial to approach meditation as a collaborative endeavor. Parents and caregivers should engage in open and honest conversations with children, listening attentively to their thoughts, concerns, and preferences regarding meditation. By including them in the decision-making process, children feel respected and valued, fostering a deeper sense of ownership over their meditation practice.

MODELING POSITIVE BEHAVIOR: LEADING BY EXAMPLE

Embracing Collaboration in Teaching Meditation to Children

In our mission to teach meditation to children, it is vital to embrace a collaborative approach that honors their choices and preferences. By engaging in open and honest conversations, parents and caregivers create a space where children's voices are heard and respected. In this chapter, we will explore the importance of collaboration, active listening, and decision-making, enabling children to develop a deeper sense of ownership and empowerment in their meditation practice.

Creating a Collaborative Environment

To overcome power imbalances, it is crucial to approach meditation as a collaborative endeavor. Parents and caregivers should foster an environment where open communication thrives, allowing children to express their thoughts, concerns, and preferences regarding meditation. By valuing their input, children feel respected and acknowledged, creating a strong foundation for collaboration.

Active Listening and Understanding

Active listening is an essential component of collaboration. When children express their thoughts and feelings about meditation, parents and caregivers should attentively listen, seeking to understand their perspective. By demonstrating empathy and genuine interest, adults can forge a deeper connection with children and gain valuable insights into their needs and preferences.

Inclusive Decision-Making

Involving children in decision-making processes surrounding meditation empowers them and nurtures a sense of ownership. Parents and caregivers should invite children to actively participate in discussions about meditation techniques, duration, and other relevant aspects. By considering their choices and preferences, children become active participants in shaping their meditation practice.

. . .

Honoring Choices and Preferences

Respecting and honoring children's choices and preferences is vital in promoting collaboration. Parents and caregivers should create an environment where children's decisions regarding meditation are valued. This may include allowing them to choose a meditation space, select a preferred technique, or decide on a suitable time for practice. By honoring their choices, children gain a sense of autonomy and feel empowered in their meditation journey.

Adapting and Evolving Together

Collaboration in meditation is a dynamic process that evolves over time. Parents and caregivers should remain open to adapt and adjust their approach based on children's feedback and evolving needs. As children grow and develop, their preferences and interests may change. By maintaining open lines of communication and embracing flexibility, adults can ensure that the meditation practice remains meaningful and engaging for children.

In this chapter, we have explored the importance of collaboration, active listening, and inclusive decision-making in teaching meditation to children. By creating a collaborative environment, honoring choices and preferences, and fostering adaptability, parents and caregivers empower children to take ownership of their meditation practice. As we progress, we will delve deeper into specific techniques and activities that further enhance collaboration, enabling children to embark on a transformative meditation journey that aligns with their unique needs and aspirations.

CREATING A SAFE SPACE: TRUST AND OPEN COMMUNICATION

Cultivating Trust and Open Communication in Teaching Meditation to Children

In our journey to teach meditation to children, the establishment of trust and open communication holds great significance. Parents and caregivers must create a safe space where children feel comfortable expressing their thoughts and concerns about meditation. By fostering dialogue, actively listening, and validating their emotions, we can bridge the gap between resistance and acceptance. In this chapter, we will explore strategies to cultivate trust and open communication, nurturing a supportive environment for children to embrace meditation.

Creating a Safe Haven

To address power imbalances, it is crucial to create a safe haven where children feel secure in expressing their feelings and concerns about meditation. Parents and caregivers should foster an environment of trust, understanding, and acceptance. By assuring children that their thoughts and emotions are valued and respected, they will feel more inclined to engage in open communication.

Encouraging Dialogue

Encouraging open dialogue is key to establishing trust and understanding. Create opportunities for children to freely express their thoughts, questions, and concerns about meditation. Encourage them to share their experiences, both positive and challenging, and provide a listening ear without judgment. By actively engaging in conversation, parents and caregivers demonstrate their commitment to understanding children's perspectives.

Active Listening and Validation

Active listening plays a crucial role in open communication. When children express their thoughts and emotions about meditation, parents and caregivers should attentively listen and seek to understand their point of view. Validate their emotions by acknowledging and empathizing with their experiences. Letting them know that their feelings are valid and important fosters a sense of trust and encourages further communication.

Resolving Conflicts with Compassion

Conflicts or disagreements may arise in the context of meditation. It is essential to approach these situations with compassion and understanding. Encourage open discussion about challenges and work together to find resolutions. By involving children in problem-solving processes, they feel empowered and develop a sense of ownership over their meditation practice.

Nurturing Emotional Well-being

Creating a safe space for open communication also nurtures children's emotional well-being. Meditation can bring forth a range of emotions, and it is vital for parents and caregivers to support children in navigating these feelings. Provide reassurance, offer guidance, and emphasize that it is normal to experience a variety of emotions during meditation. By nurturing their emotional well-being, children feel more comfortable and willing to engage in the practice.

. . .

In this chapter, we have explored strategies to cultivate trust and open communication in teaching meditation to children. By creating a safe haven, encouraging dialogue, actively listening, validating emotions, resolving conflicts with compassion, and nurturing emotional well-being, parents and caregivers foster an environment where children can freely express their thoughts and concerns about meditation. As we move forward, we will delve deeper into specific techniques and activities that further enhance trust, communication, and emotional well-being, promoting a harmonious and fulfilling meditation journey for children.

FLEXIBILITY AND ADAPTABILITY: TAILORING MEDITATION TO INDIVIDUAL NEEDS

Embracing Flexibility and Adaptability in Teaching Meditation to Children

In our pursuit of teaching meditation to children, it is important to acknowledge the uniqueness of each child. To create an inclusive and empowering experience, parents and caregivers should embrace flexibility and adaptability. By tailoring the practice to the child's individual needs, preferences, and developmental stage, we can ensure that meditation resonates with them on a personal level. In this chapter, we will explore the significance of customization, from adjusting session durations to exploring diverse meditation techniques, in fostering a meaningful and enriching meditation journey for children.

Recognizing Individuality

Children are unique individuals, each with their own set of needs, preferences, and developmental stages. Recognizing and respecting these individual differences is key to tailoring meditation effectively. By understanding that what works for one child may not work for another, parents and caregivers can adopt a flexible mindset that promotes inclusivity and engagement.

Adjusting Session Duration

One way to customize meditation is by adjusting the duration of sessions. Younger children may have shorter attention spans and benefit from brief, focused meditation practices. As they grow older, their ability to engage in longer sessions may increase. By adapting the length of meditation to suit the child's age and capabilities, we create an environment that encourages their active participation.

Exploring Meditation Techniques

There are various meditation techniques available, each with its own unique qualities and benefits. Tailoring the practice involves exploring and experimenting with different techniques to find the ones that resonate with the child. Some children may prefer guided meditations, while others might enjoy mindful breathing or visualization exercises. By providing exposure to different techniques and observing the child's response, parents and caregivers can identify the approaches that best suit their individual needs.

Adapting to Developmental Stages

Children's meditation needs to evolve as they progress through different developmental stages. Younger children may require more interactive and playful meditation activities to hold their attention. As they grow older, they may benefit from practices that encourage self-reflection and introspection. By adapting the meditation approach to align with the child's developmental stage, parents and caregivers can ensure that the practice remains engaging and relevant throughout their growth.

Encouraging Expression and Feedback

Tailoring meditation requires open communication and feedback from the child. Encourage children to express their thoughts, emotions, and preferences regarding meditation practice. Actively listen to their feedback and incorporate their ideas when appropriate. By involving them in the customization process, children feel empowered and invested in their own meditation journey.

In this chapter, we have explored the importance of flexibility and adaptability in teaching meditation to children. By recognizing individuality, adjusting session durations, exploring meditation techniques, adapting to developmental stages, and encouraging expression and feedback, parents and caregivers create a customized and meaningful meditation experience for children. As we move forward, we will delve deeper into specific techniques and activities that cater to individual needs, fostering a lifelong practice that supports their growth and well-being.

CONCLUSION

NURTURING EMPOWERMENT AND GROWTH IN TEACHING MEDITATION TO CHILDREN

Throughout this book, we have explored the common challenges faced by parents and caregivers when teaching meditation to children and provided strategies to overcome them. In our journey, we discovered that addressing power imbalances is crucial in creating a harmonious and fulfilling meditation practice for children.

By fostering a collaborative approach, we empower children to be active participants in their meditation journey. Honoring their choices and preferences allows them to develop a sense of ownership and control, leading to a more engaged and enthusiastic practice. Modeling positive behavior and showcasing the benefits of meditation inspire children to embrace it willingly and wholeheartedly.

Creating a safe space for open communication is essential. By listening attentively, validating their emotions, and nurturing trust, parents, and caregivers encourage children to express their thoughts and concerns about meditation freely. This open dialogue bridges the gap between resistance and acceptance, paving the way for a deeper understanding and connection.

Recognizing that each child is unique, we emphasized the importance of flexibility and adaptability. By tailoring the meditation practice to their individual needs, preferences, and developmental stages, we ensure that it resonates with them on a personal level. Adjusting session durations, exploring diverse meditation techniques, and adapting to their growth foster an inclusive and enriching experience.

As we conclude this book, let us strive to create an environment where meditation becomes a source of empowerment, self-discovery, and inner peace for children of all ages. By addressing power imbalances, nurturing collaboration, and adapting to their individuality, we enable children to embrace meditation as a lifelong tool for well-being and personal growth.

May this journey of teaching meditation to children be filled with joy, growth, and profound connections. Together, let us inspire the next generation to cultivate mindfulness, resilience, and a deep sense of inner peace.

CHAPTER 17
TEACHING MEDITATION TO CHILDREN FROM DIVERSE CULTURES
Q&A

TEACHING Meditation to Children from Diverse Cultures

Q: Why is cultural sensitivity important when teaching meditation to children?

A: Cultural sensitivity is crucial when teaching meditation to children because cultural diversity and individual beliefs play a significant role in shaping the practice. Each child comes from a unique cultural background with its own traditions, values, and spiritual customs. It is essential for parents and teachers to recognize and respect these differences to ensure the meditation instructions are inclusive, appropriate, and meaningful for the child. Being culturally sensitive prevents misunderstandings, avoids conflicts with family beliefs, and enables the child to fully engage with mindfulness in a way that honors their cultural identity.

Q: How can I learn about a child's cultural background and beliefs?

A: Taking time to understand the child's cultural background is the first step. Have open discussions with the child and their family to learn about cultural views, traditions, and spiritual practices related to meditation. Be mindful of how meditation is perceived within different cultures – practices like chanting or certain postures may have more or less significance. Observance of cultural holidays and events can provide insights into beliefs. Visit cultural centers and places of worship to deepen your knowledge. Read books on meditation traditions across cultures. Approach learning with an open and curious mindset, avoiding assumptions. Let the child's perspectives guide you.

Q: What is an inclusive and culturally sensitive environment for teaching meditation?

A: An inclusive meditation environment values diversity and adapts to the needs of each child. It ensures children of all backgrounds feel respected, heard, and represented. Set ground rules of respectful sharing and open dialogue. Display cultural symbols like artwork, flags, or decorations to acknowledge heritage. Share stories about meditation practices from various cultures. Tailor language and examples in your instructions to resonate across cultures. Welcome children to share cultural wisdom. Foster togetherness while honoring each child's identity. Adapt techniques to accommodate cultural practices and beliefs. Cultivate an atmosphere of empathy, understanding, and belonging.

Q: How can I adapt meditation techniques for cultural alignment?

A: Aligning techniques to a child's culture can make meditation more relevant. For children from Indigenous cultures, incorporate nature-connected practices outdoors. Use tribal stories and ancestral wisdom in guided imagery. For Asian children, teach movement meditations like tai chi, or introduce meaningful mantras. For Muslim students, discuss meditative elements in the salah prayer. Work collaboratively with children and families to modify techniques in culturally appropriate ways. Be flexible and open to trying new approaches to find common ground.

Q: What cultural considerations apply to meditation storytelling?

A: Stories can make meditation relatable, but choose narratives that align with cultural backgrounds. Draw from fables and folklore from each child's heritage. For a Christian child, use parables as examples in guided imagery. For an Indian child, share tales that reference Hindu teachings. Adapt stories to resonate across cultures, too – conveying universal values of compassion and wisdom. Avoid appropriating stories not belonging to a child's background. Do research to retell tales respectfully. When possible, invite family and community members to share meaningful stories from their cultures.

Q: How can I facilitate discussions about cultural beliefs related to meditation?

A: Facilitating open discussions creates a safe space for children to explore cultural perspectives. Set expectations for respectful sharing of thoughts and questions. Be aware of cultural differences in communication styles – some children may be more or less comfortable speaking up. Provide writing or drawing prompts for more introverted children to express themselves. Share your own learning journey navigating cultural meditative practices. Guide children to discuss both differences and commonalities across cultures. Foster an atmosphere of genuine curiosity, empathy, and appreciation for diverse viewpoints.

Q: What if my student's family does not support meditation?

A: Respect the family's position and explore alternatives that align with their values. Mindfulness does not have to mean formal meditation. Seek compatible activities like mindful art, journaling, or time in nature that nurture awareness. Communicate with compassion and sensitivity. Ask how to find common ground respectfully. The goal is to support the child's well-being in a culturally aligned way. Build trust through ongoing dialogue with the family.

Q: How can I be culturally responsive when leading group meditation?

A: Incorporate cultural inclusivity into group meditation sessions through music, mantras, or readings. Invite children to share culturally important practices. Adapt guided imagery using diverse cultural symbols and imagery. Provide supportive cushions or mats to accommodate different postures. Offer modifications for practices that may not align with certain beliefs. Check-in with students to ensure techniques resonate across cultures. As the teacher, educate yourself on cultural protocols related to touch or personal space. Foster a welcoming circle where all backgrounds are celebrated.

Q: Why is it important to embrace diversity in meditation teachings?

A: Embracing diversity makes meditation more enriching by integrating wisdom from different cultures. It enables children to connect meditation with their cultural identity. Valuing inclusivity promotes empathy, equality, and harmony in the classroom and community. Respecting diverse viewpoints nurtures open-mindedness. Children learn from each other's cultural perspectives, fostering mutual understanding. A culturally responsive approach makes mindfulness accessible and beneficial to all students. When meditation honors their backgrounds, children gain tools to navigate life's challenges in healthy ways.

Q: How can I continue expanding my cultural awareness as a meditation teacher?

A: Cultural learning is an ongoing process. Immerse yourself in books, films, and events celebrating your students' cultures. Visit local places of worship and cultural centers. Follow thought leaders from diverse backgrounds. Examine your own assumptions and blind spots. Ask families to review your curriculum and teaching materials to ensure alignment with cultural needs. Solicit student feedback through surveys or discussions on your cultural responsiveness. Seek training in areas like non-violent communication across cultures. Stay open and humble, continuously striving to understand diverse cultural experiences and apply that knowledge to your teachings with care.

In summary, teaching meditation to children in a culturally sensitive manner requires dedication to understanding backgrounds, adapting techniques, facilitating discussions, collaborating with families, modifying group sessions, embracing inclusivity, and continuously expanding our awareness as educators. When mindfulness instruction honors and aligns with a child's cultural identity, it can become a profound practice that supports their lifelong well-being, self-discovery, and sense of belonging.

Q: How can I adapt guided meditation visualizations for cultural alignment?

. . .

A: Guided visualization is a powerful mindfulness technique, but imagery should reflect the child's cultural background. First, research symbols, archetypes, and folklore from the child's heritage to inform culturally relevant visuals. Incorporate scenery and architecture that the child relates to. Use names and terms familiar in their native language to create a sense of connection. Feature influential historical and cultural figures that inspire the child. Adapt metaphors and similes using examples from their cultural stories and fables. Offer options for the child to visualize a cultural ritual, celebration, or rite of passage. Avoid appropriating or misrepresenting cultural elements in the visualization. Work collaboratively with the child or family to ensure it resonates with their background.

Q: What modifications can make meditation more accessible across physical abilities and needs?

A: Meditation should accommodate children of all physical abilities. Provide supportive cushions, chairs, or assistive devices to facilitate comfortable postures. Offer alternatives to sitting or lying down, like mindful standing or walking. Adapt hand gestures or mudras to suit dexterity levels. For visual impairments, guide detailed visualizations and focus on auditory, tactile, or kinetic cues. Allow fidgeting aids to channel restless energy. If needed, shorten the session length or intersperse periods of meditation with movement. Check frequently for discomfort and invite feedback on any modifications required. The practices can flex to the child's abilities while still fostering mindfulness.

Q: How can I reassure a neurodivergent child who is anxious about "meditating correctly"?

A: Neurodivergent children may feel added anxiety about meditating "right." Emphasize there are many ways to practice mindfulness that work for them. Avoid language that pressures perfect stillness or silence. Encourage them to explore different postures and techniques to find what feels calming. Reassure them that fidgeting or adjusting is okay. Suggest focusing on a soothing object or sound if their thoughts feel too busy. Remind them the goal is simply to tune into the present, not to force their mind to do anything unnatural. Patience and compassion for oneself are key. They cannot make mistakes if they meditate in ways that feel good to their body and mind.

Q: What considerations should be made for children with religious beliefs about meditation?

A: Respect a child's religious views about meditation by taking time to understand their faith's principles and practices related to mindfulness. Some may have specific ritualized meditations. Avoid contradicting or misrepresenting their beliefs. Explain meditation can coexist with and even enhance religious rituals. Incorporate elements from their tradition, like prayers or texts. Collaborate to create secular practices that align with principles of their faith about peace, compassion, etc. Allow children to share how their religion guides their spiritual growth. Never force participation in practices contrary to their beliefs. With open dialogue and adaptability, meditation can support a child's religious and spiritual journey.

Q: How can mindfulness help children manage learning differences like ADHD and dyslexia?

A: Mindfulness practices can support children with learning differences such as ADHD and dyslexia. For ADHD, meditation cultivates skills for managing distraction, improving concentration, and controlling impulses. Make sessions interactive with guided imagery, movement, or fidget aids. Support dyslexic children by providing auditory instructions and avoiding long readings. Use visualization to reduce anxiety and build self-esteem. Practicing mindfulness, children learn techniques to self-regulate emotions, channel focus, and gain greater agency over the mind and body. This empowers them as learners. An inclusive, adaptive approach makes mindfulness accessible as a tool for children to flourish despite differences.

Q: What are some best practices for teaching mindful eating to children with food restrictions?

A: When guiding mindful eating practices, always accommodate food restrictions. For children with allergies or intolerances, provide alternative ingredients they can safely experience, like wheat-free crackers or dairy-free chocolate. Substitute visually similar items, like rice cakes, for bread. Create non-food sensory experiences involving aroma, sound, or texture. Avoid triggering self-judgment around restrictions - remind children food has no moral value. Help them cultivate gratitude for foods nourishing their body rather than deprivation. With creativity and compassion, mindful eating can teach invaluable lessons about sensory awareness, self-care, and listening to one's needs, inclusive of every child.

Q: How can I make meditation more accessible for children from underserved communities?

A: Children from underserved communities may face barriers to engaging in mindfulness. Offer sessions at flexible times to accommodate family schedules. Provide transportation, resources, or scholarships if needed. Hold sessions at accessible community venues. Make practices relatable by using familiar examples and language. Adapt techniques to be simple and low-cost, requiring minimal supplies. Acknowledge and validate the challenges they face. Practice compassion and avoid judgment. Ensure your instructions and guidance resonate with their experiences and culture. With patience and understanding, meditation can provide essential tools for resilience and self-care to children who stand to benefit profoundly from its gifts.

In summary, cultural sensitivity, inclusivity, and adaptability in meditation instruction enable all children - regardless of background, beliefs, or abilities - to receive the benefits of mindfulness in an appropriate and meaningful way. When we honor each child's uniqueness, meditation becomes a unifying practice, cultivating mutual understanding and shared well-being while allowing their inner wisdom, strengths, and beauty to flourish.

PART 6: ADDRESSING QUESTIONS AND CHALLENGES

Conclusion and Next Steps: Embracing Mindfulness in Everyday Life
- Afterword
- Also by Manon Doucet
- References

CHAPTER 18
CONCLUSION AND NEXT STEPS: EMBRACING MINDFULNESS IN EVERYDAY LIFE
CONCLUSION: CONTINUING OUR MINDFULNESS JOURNEY

AS WE REACH the close of this book, it is a fitting moment to pause and reflect on our shared journey of nurturing mindfulness and meditation in children. We have now explored a wealth of techniques, activities, and guidance tailored for children across different ages and developmental stages.

This final chapter provides an opportunity to revisit key lessons, consider how to integrate mindfulness into everyday life, and outline the next steps to continue deepening our practice together with children. By summarizing the core concepts and looking ahead, we can sustain our momentum and commitment on this unfolding path.

Understanding Emotions with Compassion

A consistent thread throughout this book has been the essential ability to tune into emotions with compassionate awareness—our own and our child's inner experiences. By teaching children to identify and name their emotions, we help them make sense of their inner world. Seeing feelings clearly without judgment fosters emotional intelligence, communication skills, resilience, and empathy.

We have shared strategies to create a nurturing environment where children's emotions are validated and supported, not criticized or punished. Whether through stories, role-playing, or mindful listening, the goal has been to develop emotional awareness as a valuable life skill. Our children come to understand that all emotions are acceptable, even if certain behaviors may be redirected. This emotional foundation strengthens children to navigate life's ups and downs with wisdom and grace.

Adapting Mindfulness to Developmental Needs

Given each child's unique developmental trajectory, we have emphasized tailoring techniques to align with their evolving capacities and needs. For example, younger children thrive with brief, play-based practices while teens benefit from longer silent meditation and self-reflection.

Modifying activities based on attention span, comprehension level, motor skills, and interests allows children to integrate mindfulness at their own pace. Customizing our approach reinforces that mindfulness is their personal journey, not a rigid, one-size-fits-all system. Adaptability combined with consistency and patience enables children to fully blossom in their own time.

Weaving Mindfulness Into Daily Life

While formal meditation sessions provide dedicated space to cultivate awareness, mindfulness is ultimately meant to infuse all of life. We have explored simple ways to incorporate mindful moments throughout the day, making it a natural habit rather than isolated practice.

Tuning into the senses during routine activities—listening intently during story time, noticing thoughts and emotions during the school day, savoring a mindful meal—helps children step out of auto-pilot and into conscious presence. Embedding these reminders to return to the here and now transforms mindfulness into an ever-accessible lifeline, allowing children to refocus their attention and anchor themselves in peace.

The Importance of Family and Community

Our shared exploration has reinforced that imparting mindfulness to children is not a solo endeavor. Having the support of family and community provides a nurturing ecosystem for mindfulness to flourish. Children absorb mindfulness by observing those around them practice it in everyday life. Shared activities weave mindfulness into the fabric of family connection.

By cultivating mindful communication, modulating our own reactions, making space for family practice, and openly discussing experiences, we model mindfulness beyond superficial acts. Children come to see that mindfulness means living with integrity. Our journey together casts ripples of awareness that uplift our whole family system.

LOOKING AHEAD WITH MINDFUL INTENTION

As we integrate mindfulness more fully into our family's rhythms and routines moving forward, here are some intentions that may guide our continued path:

- Make time each day, even 10 minutes, for simple practices together. Consistency and repetition instill lifelong habits.

- Help each other gently return to the present moment whenever distracted. Compassion begets compassion.

- Remember there is no perfect way. Meet yourselves and each child where you are with patience. Progress comes slowly.

- Share positive experiences but let go of expectations. Each journey is unique. Trust in their inner wisdom.

- Continue to learn and explore new mindfulness resources together. This is a lifelong adventure. We grow together.

CONCLUSION: A MINDFULNESS SEED PLANTED WITH LOVE

In many ways, imparting mindfulness to our children is like planting a precious seed while trusting in its innate perfection. We do our best to give it nourishment, sunlight, and care. We understand it may sprout differently than we imagined. Yet if we come from faith in its inner potential, this seed will naturally grow strong roots and blossom.

Likewise, if we approach mindfulness with unwavering love and compassion for our children, this clear intention shines through. It gives children fertile ground to connect with their own inner wisdom and compassion. In time, mindfulness matures from our guidance to become their natural way of life, enriching all they do.

While each family's mindfulness journey will have its own rhythm, together, we have built a foundation. May our children savor this gift of presence to guide them through both joys and sorrows. And may they plant new seeds that spread mindfulness, inner peace, and loving awareness for generations to come.

AFTERWORD

A Parting Reflection

As I reflect back on the journey of writing this book, I am filled with gratitude and optimism about the future. Despite the inevitable challenges, imparting the gifts of mindfulness meditation to our children is a worthy and vital endeavor.

The pages you have read contain the distilled insights from my decades of personal practice, teaching, and researching this profound subject. But beyond the techniques, stories, and activities, a few themes stand out as the secret seeds that can help mindfulness blossom in our children's lives.

First and foremost is recognizing the power of mindfulness already residing within each child, waiting to be unlocked. Meditation is merely a tool to help them discover their natural inner wisdom, emotional awareness, and stillness. When we approach children with this empowering perspective, they bloom from the inside out.

Equally important is meeting them where they are with gentleness and understanding. Progress happens slowly and organically. The fruits of meditation require patient nurturing and tender care. Each child's inner terrain is unique. Trust the process.

Though mindfulness offers countless benefits, it is essential we present it to children in ways that are imaginative, sensory, and hands-on. When practices resonate with their playful spirit, meditation becomes an adventure rather than an obligation.

Of course, our own modeling of mindful behaviors provides a fertile example for kids to follow. They absorb far more from who we are than what we say. By living mindfully, we show children it can infuse all of life.

While techniques, tools, and teaching strategies have been provided, what matters most is consistency. Regular short practices of even a few minutes are infinitely more valuable than occasional long sessions. Gentle daily effort compounds over time.

Rather than a rigid protocol, mindfulness is meant to spread like a soft mist over all moments of our days. We naturally create opportunities to weave mindful pauses into ordinary routines when it becomes our way of being.

In this journey, we must honor each child's unique inner landscape. There is no singular roadmap; stay open and meet them where they are. Nurture their mindfulness in ways that align with their needs and interests.

Patience and self-compassion are essential nutrients for this practice to take root. Children require a non-judgmental space as their skills develop through gentle repetition. Trust this unfolding.

By embracing these secrets - the power within, compassionate patience, creative play, mindful modeling, routine consistency, flexible integration, deep listening, and self-acceptance - meditation becomes an effortless inner resource our children can tap into for life. More than any specific technique, these ingredients allow mindfulness to flourish.

As I close this book, I bow to the inner radiance within all children, waiting patiently to be illuminated. May the parents, caregivers, and teachers who nurture our future generations do so with all the love, wisdom, and devotion they can offer. When we honor the wholeness already residing within each child, they bloom beyond our wildest imaginings. This is the quiet miracle mindfulness reveals.

ALSO BY MANON DOUCET

The best meditation for women

REFERENCES

McCarthy, E., & Floss, T. T. a. M. (2021). *Mental Floss: The Curious Reader Journal for Book Lovers.* Simon and Schuster.

Hayman, S., & Coleman, J. (2016b). *Parents and digital technology: How to Raise the Connected Generation.* Routledge.

Clauss-Ehlers, C. S., Sood, A. B., & Weist, M. D. (2020). *Social justice for children and young people: International Perspectives.* Cambridge University Press.

Issues in Pediatric and Adolescent Medicine Research and Practice: 2011 edition. (2012). ScholarlyEditions.

Alishah, Z. (2023). *Parenting with Positive Thinking: Unlock the Potential of Positive Parenting.* Balboa Press.

Sanders, M. R., & Morawska, A. (2018). *Handbook of Parenting and Child Development across the Lifespan.* Springer.

The advocate. (2001).

Eddy, M., & Moradian, A. L. (2018). ChildhoodNature in Motion: The Ground for Learning. In *Springer international handbooks of Education* (pp. 1–24). https://doi.org/10.1007/978-3-319-51949-4_97-2

Bethune, A. (2023). *Wellbeing in the primary classroom: The updated guide to teaching happiness and positive mental health.* Bloomsbury Publishing.

Welch, C. (2020). *The gift of presence: a mindfulness guide for women.* Scribe Publications.

Bar-On, R., Maree, K., & Elias, M. J. (2007). *Educating people to be emotionally intelligent.* Praeger.

Kenrick, J. (2018). *Creating new families: Therapeutic Approaches to Fostering, Adoption and Kinship Care.* Routledge.

Issues in Clinical Psychology, Psychiatry, and Counseling: 2011 edition. (2012). ScholarlyEditions.

Issues in Pediatric and Adolescent Medicine Research and Practice: 2011 edition. (Stanley et al., 2018)

Stanley, S., Purser, R. E., & Singh, N. N. (2018). *Handbook of Ethical Foundations of Mindfulness.* Springer.

Congress, U. S. (1974). *Congressional record: Proceedings and Debates of the . . . Congress.*

Hay, L. (2016). *Mirror work: 21 Days to Heal Your Life.* Hay House, Inc.

Chen, Q., Yang, W., Li, W., Wei, D., Li, H., Qiao, L., Zhang, Q., & Qiu, J. (2014). Association of creative achievement with cognitive flexibility by a combined voxel-based morphometry and resting-state functional connectivity study. *NeuroImage*, 102, 474–483. https://doi.org/10.1016/j.neuroimage.2014.08.008

Goleman, D. (2006). *Emotional intelligence: Why It Can Matter More Than IQ*. Bantam.

Newman, B. M., & Newman, P. R. (2017). *Development Through Life: A Psychosocial approach*. Cengage Learning.

Medicine, N. a. O. S. E. A., Education, D. O. B. a. S. S. A., Families, B. O. C. Y. A., & Children, C. O. S. T. P. O. Y. (2016). *Parenting matters: Supporting Parents of Children Ages 0-8*. National Academies Press.

Naidoo, U. (2020). *This is your brain on food: An Indispensable Guide to the Surprising Foods that Fight Depression, Anxiety, PTSD, OCD, ADHD, and More*. Hachette UK.

Siegel, D. J. (2015). *The Developing Mind, second edition: How Relationships and the Brain Interact to Shape Who We Are.* Guilford Publications.

Bratton, S. C., & Landreth, G. L. (2019). *Child-Parent Relationship Therapy (CPRT) Treatment Manual: An Evidence-Based 10-Session Filial Therapy Model.* Routledge.

Arbitrament, S. I. (2019). *Sun Tzu: In the Midst of Chaos There Is Also Opportunity.*

Gullotta, T. P., & Adams, G. R. (2007). *Handbook of Adolescent Behavioral Problems: Evidence-Based Approaches to Prevention and Treatment.* Springer Science & Business Media.

Medicine, N. a. O. S. E. A., Division, H. a. M., Education, D. O. B. a. S. S. A., Families, B. O. C. Y. A., & Applications, C. O. T. N. a. S. S. O. a. D. a. I. (2019). *The promise of adolescence: Realizing Opportunity for All Youth.* National Academies Press.

Tang, Y. (2017). *The neuroscience of mindfulness meditation: How the Body and Mind Work Together to Change Our Behaviour.* Springer.

Ninivaggi, F. J. (2019). *Learned mindfulness: Physician* Council, N. R., Medicine, I. O., Families, B. O. C. Y. A., & Success, C. O. T. S. O. C. B. T. a. 8. D. a. B. T. F. F. (2015). *Transforming the workforce for children birth through age 8: A Unifying Foundation.* National Academies Press.

Tang, Y. (2017b). *The neuroscience of mindfulness meditation: How the Body and Mind Work Together to Change Our Behaviour.* Springer.

Greene, J. D., Morrison, I., & Seligman, M. E. P. (2016). *Positive Neuroscience.* Oxford University Press.

Leary, M. R., & Hoyle, R. H. (2013). *Handbook of Individual Differences in Social Behavior.* Guilford Publications.

Niemiec, R. M. (2023). *Mindfulness and character strengths: A Practitioner's Guide to MBSP.* Hogrefe Publishing GmbH.

Keengwe, J. (2022). *Handbook of Research on Active Learning and Student Engagement in Higher Education.* IGI Global.

Fisk, G. D. (2018). *Slides for students: The Effective Use of Powerpoint in Education.*

Bullock, B. G. (2016). *Mindful relationships: Seven Skills for Success.* Jessica Kingsley Publishers.

Arden, J. B. (2010). *Rewire your brain: Think Your Way to a Better Life.* John Wiley & Sons.

Eisendrath, S. J. (2016). *Mindfulness-Based cognitive therapy: Innovative Applications.* Springer.

Langland-Hassan, P., & Vicente, A. (2018). *Inner speech: New Voices.* Oxford University Press, USA.

Yogman, M. W., Garner, A. S., Hutchinson, J., Hirsh-Pasek, K., & Golinkoff, R. M. (2018). The Power of Play: A pediatric role in enhancing development in young children. *Pediatrics, 142*(3). https://doi.org/10.1542/peds.2018-2058

Bohr, A., & Memarzadeh, K. (2020). *Artificial intelligence in healthcare*. Academic Press.

Douglass, F. (2018). *The hypocrisy of American slavery*. Createspace Independent Publishing Platform.

Stewart, J. (2021). *The organization leaves no traces*.

Arden, J. B. (2010b). *Rewire your brain: Think Your Way to a Better Life*. John Wiley & Sons.

Starko, A. J. (2021). *Creativity in the classroom: Schools of Curious Delight*. Routledge.

Dupeyrat, L., & Bernard, J. (2019). *Meditation for Kids: How to Clear Your Head and Calm Your Mind*. Shambhala Publications.

Paley, V. G. (2009). *A child's work: The Importance of Fantasy Play*. University of Chicago Press.

Stewart, W. (2017). *Mindful kids: 50 Mindfulness Activities for Kindness, Focus, and Calm.*

Petts, R. J. (2019). *Religion and family life.* MDPI.

Cantor, P., & Osher, D. (2021). *The science of learning and development: Enhancing the Lives of All Young People.* Routledge.

Williams, J. M. G., Teasdale, J. D., Segal, Z. V., & Kabat-Zinn, J. (2012). *The Mindful Way through Depression: Freeing Yourself from Chronic Unhappiness.* Guilford Press.

Sweet, S. D., & Miles, B. S. (2021). *King Calm: Mindful Gorilla in the City.* American Psychological Association.

Medicine, N. a. O. S. E. A., Division, H. a. M., & Practice, B. O. P. H. a. P. H. (2020). *Brain health across the life span: Proceedings of a Workshop.* National Academies Press.

Allen, J. L., Hawes, D. J., & Essau, C. A. (2021). *Family-Based Intervention for Child and Adolescent Mental Health: A Core Competencies Approach.* Cambridge University Press.

Fancourt, D., & Finn, S. (2019). *What is the evidence on the role of the arts in improving health and Well-Being.*

Fancourt, D., & Finn, S. (2019). *What is the evidence on the role of the arts in improving health and Well-Being.*

Ford, M. E., & Smith, P. R. (2020). *Motivating self and others: Thriving with Social Purpose, Life Meaning, and the Pursuit of Core Personal Goals.* Cambridge University Press.

Well, T. (2022). *Mirror meditation: The Power of Neuroscience and Self-Reflection to Overcome Self-Criticism, Gain Confidence, and See Yourself with Compassion.* New Harbinger Publications.

Hampton, A. (2023). *Facing fear: The Journey to Mature Courage in Risk and Persecution.* William Carey Publishing.

Herman, P. M., & Coulter, I. D. (2015). *Complementary and Alternative Medicine, Professions Or Modalities?: Policy Implications for Coverage, Licensure, Scope of Practice, Institutional Privileges, and Research.* Rand Corporation.

Brackett, M. (2019). *Permission to feel: Unlock the power of emotions to help yourself and your children thrive.* Hachette UK.

Beng, T. S. (2023). *The little Handbook of Mindfulness.* Partridge Publishing Singapore.

Kirmayer, L. J., Worthman, C. M., Kitayama, S., Lemelson, R., & Cummings, C. (2020). *Culture, mind, and brain: Emerging Concepts, Models, and Applications.* Cambridge University Press.

Cantor, P., & Osher, D. (2021b). *The science of learning and development: Enhancing the Lives of All Young People.* Routledge.

A SPECIAL NOTE FROM MANON DOUCET

Hello, dear reader!

First and foremost, **thank you**. By diving into the pages of my book, you've allowed my words, my heart, and my imagination to become a part of your world. For that, I'm endlessly grateful.

Did this tale whisk you away on an adventure, spark an emotion, or leave an impression? If so, I'd love to hear about it!

Here's how you can share your thoughts:
    Revisit the platform where you found this book. Be it Amazon, Kobo, Barns and Nobles, Apple Books, Google Play or any other cozy corner of the literary world.

Remember, your insights might be the guiding star for another reader in search of their next read!

Click 'Submit'. Just like that, you've made a difference. Your voice might inspire someone else to embark on the same journey you did.

Your reflections not only light the way for future readers but also warm the hearts of authors like me, encouraging us to keep dreaming, writing, and sharing. It's a beautiful ripple effect, and it starts with you.

From the bottom of my heart, thank you for sharing this literary voyage with me. Here's to many more tales, adventures, and moments shared through the magic of words!

With warmth and gratitude,

Manon Doucet

ABOUT THE AUTHOR

Manon is a vibrant and complex person, offering a distinct viewpoint on personal growth through the prism of art and human connection. Drawing upon her own rich life experiences, she uses the power of narrative to share and inspire and encourages others to do the same. A seasoned educator, she has leveraged her skills to create engaging literature that fuels the curious minds of young readers and instills in them an enduring love for books. She firmly believes in the importance of taking personal time and cherishing moments with children.

Wearing many hats as a life coach, natural health enthusiast, artist, and published author, Manon serves as a guiding beacon for families on their life's voyage. She assists them in managing life's ebbs and flows, fortifying their familial relationships, and unveiling the awe-inspiring journey of self-discovery. Her writings are imbued with emotional depth and sincerity, mirroring her zeal for life and her commitment to ushering in a positive change in her environment.

Whether it's through the lens of her camera or her role as a spiritual guide, Manon's pursuits are characterized by an unwavering dedication to empowering individuals, nurturing personal growth, and fostering a sense of connectedness. She sees beauty and potential in everyone she encounters, and her efforts are geared toward bringing this vision to life. Her multifaceted personality, combined with her diverse talents and passions, enables her to make a truly meaningful impact on the world.

www.ingramcontent.com/pod-product-compliance
Lightning Source LLC
Chambersburg PA
CBHW071214080526
44587CB00013BA/1370